Guidelines for Mystical Prayer

Guidelines
for
Mystical Prayer

Ruth Burrows

Paulist Press
New York / Mahwah, NJ

First published by Bruns and Oates
(Bloomsbury Publishing Plc) in 1976.

Seventh impression 1984
This edition published 2007 and reprinted 2017.

Cover illustration by Beata Becla / Shutterstock.com

Library of Congress Control Number: 2016962649

ISBN 978-0-8091-5358-9

Paulist Press, Inc.
997 MacArthur Boulevard
Mahwah, New Jersey 07430

www.paulistpress.com

Printed and bound in the United States of America

CONTENTS

To K
and many others
known and unknown
whom I love
in Christ

FOREWORD

I hope that ordinary christians and others will not be frightened off this book by the fact that it is called *Guidelines for Mystical Prayer*. What on earth, one might ask, can that possibly have to do with me, floundering in a busy and harassed life punctuated by a few dull and distracted 'devotions', public or private?

The author herself wastes little time before remarking that all she is interested in is Jesus Christ, and that expressions like 'the mystical life' mean nothing to her except Jesus Christ and his life in us. She has made use of great classics of spiritual or 'mystical' literature, but she has sought in them simply our Lord and the life he leads in each and all of us (not only in our prayers but in our actions) so far as we do not bar the entrance to him.

She is convinced, and our tradition supports her, that the life of Jesus Christ is our life, and its ultimate flowering and fruiting in full holiness are the way and the goal to which God himself wishes to bring us all; it is not the preserve of the 'uncommonly good', still less of those who live in monasteries of contemplative life (as she does). 'This book', she writes, 'is meant for all', and she urges us not to be put off by the occasional technical term. Her message is, in short: 'there are no limits' to what God will do for each of us 'if only we will trust him utterly'.

This is not a book for the rigid, someone with the approach of a pre-Vatican II ecclesiastical censor who takes care to see that every half-sentence in it conforms to the teaching of 'the text-books'. It is an extremely personal expression of deep convictions, and there are certainly statements here at which the rigorous censor would be shocked. They are meant to shock, to force us to read with a christian common sense and a willingness to re-examine. If we feel with alarm: but this is surely not the 'text-book' teaching, Sister Ruth wants us to put the deeper question: but might it not be the new testament teaching? We must read her wisely, seeking the meaning which is not, nor can be, always obvious at first glance. For instance, there is a passage where she might be taken as saying that we can dispense with God as the explanation of existence. I am sure we cannot, and so is she. But in our age of science and secularisation, there may well be people who are inclined to think we can, and it is precisely for such people, among others, that she writes.

The book makes a very sharp distinction between the three 'stages' or successive states of spiritual life (what used to be called the purgative, illuminative and unitive ways). She is adamant that these — her three 'islands' — are entirely separate each from the others, though normally there is an order in which they occur — if they do all occur — in a man's spiritual development and experience here on earth. She is equally adamant — and I am very concerned to emphasise this — that at every step and stage of our pilgrimage, it is the same God, 'love divine all loves excelling', who is at work within us. Without wishing to blur any necessary distinctions, we must be certain that — whatever experience may seem to suggest — there is a profound continuity throughout the process. I think, too, we should take to heart her warning that it is particularly important we should not waste time asking ourselves what state we are traversing, which island we are on. Above all, we should not be for ever taking our spiritual temperature and feeling our mystical pulse. Indeed, is not the book's great message and summons: Forget yourself once and for all in total trust in God, who will enable you to respond to his love in his way and in his times, which may not be what you would have chosen or expected?

Some readers may at first be taken aback by the author's treatment — rough, it may seem at times — of her own beloved St Teresa of Avila. Personally, I do not object to this at all. Teresa was a vivid 'personality' and a woman of her own age and culture. We may have learnt little that Teresa did not know about Jesus Christ. But we have learnt a little about human psychology. Teresa's own disciple, the mystical doctor St John of the Cross, seems to have had some reservations about the way in which St Teresa tried to articulate a valid doctrine of the spiritual life. It is clear that Sr Ruth venerates the great Teresa, as well she might.

I am delighted, however, that she also finds herself at home with that great modern Carmelite, St Thérèse of Lisieux. Abbot Chapman once said that there was a period when good christians were plagued with temptations against hope, where-as in his day — so he thought — they were likely to be beset with temptations against faith. Thérèse was a young woman of her own age and of Chapman's, not so different in some respects from our own. You need, however, to get below the sugary surface of her language (she lived in the 'refinement' of late nineteenth-century bourgeois culture) to find the solid sub-stance of a spirituality that, like this book, bases everything on total trust and self-abandonment, and finds its essence in a pure love that is, essentially, completely free from 'the con-solations of religion'.

This book should be taken as a starting-point for thought and a vehicle of the gospel invitation: Follow me. I have found it most stimulating, and most encouraging.

B. C. Butler

INTRODUCTION

This book has been born from the womb of life. To the question 'what is it about?', I suppose several answers could be given: it is about the mystical life, infused contemplation, the three ages of the spiritual life; it is a re-interpretation of the teaching of St Teresa and St John of the Cross. But these are not the answers I want. I want to say that it is about Jesus, Jesus crucified, the wisdom of God. For mystical life, infused contemplation, these things mean absolutely nothing to me unless they mean Jesus and his life in us; Jesus who alone brings God and man together; Jesus our holiness. 'You alone are the holy one'. Although my approach to the spiritual life is a simple one, my make-up is complicated and tortuous, and therefore I have had all sorts of difficulties on the intellectual and emotional level and, for me, a theoretical problem is a practical one too. But it is of these very difficulties this book is made. At long last all has fallen into place for me and been reduced to a beautiful simplicity that my deepest heart has always known: that Jesus is everything, and that theology, the mystical life, and practical living form but one whole: Jesus first and last, Christ crucified, the wisdom and the power of God.

This heart, this innermost meaning of the mystical life, I want to show in a realistic way with reference to tradition, especially to the Carmelite writers, Teresa and John. After all, they take over the tradition, develop and give a scientific account of it. Their authority is universally recognised, their works continually read, and yet they are open to grave misunderstanding which can and does prove harmful. I want to seize on the essence of what they are saying and show what it means today, 'how it works' among ordinary people.

I am chuckling to myself at the idea of my writing on mysticism, when once I couldn't bear the word and eschewed discussion of it. But that was precisely because it seemed to me to be unrelated to Jesus, to be seen as something cultivated, a fascinating possibility, something that gave promise of a wonderful experience. This I could not bear: pseudo-mysticism, undoubtedly not the real thing. What then is true mysticism, asked my questing mind.

For years I worried so. From all I read it seemed taken for granted that unless one received mystical graces then one was a second-class citizen with a second-class ticket. I was quite sure I'd received no mystical graces; I was dry as a bone and always had been. It wasn't that I coveted the experience I read about; on the contrary it put me off, but that sort of experience seemed a hallmark of God's favour and confirmed that one was pleasing to him. Later on common-sense came to my rescue, common-sense and faith. God is good, is faithful. If I trust him and surrender to him in whatever way I see, then I need have no worries; somehow I began to suspect that the answer was that somewhere along the line was a big mistake, a big misunderstanding; I sought to find it.

I was not left to search alone. God sent Claire to me. I had been told her way of prayer was extraordinary, that in fact she was a mystic. I had become sceptical by now, as I have said, having come up a lot against what was classed as mystical. So up went my antennae and, to change the metaphor, I sniffed her suspiciously from head to foot. My scepticism was disarmed, my prejudice destroyed. 'There is nothing pseudo here', I thought, 'every note rings true. Here is profound humility and total surrender to God. Only God matters to this woman. She is immersed in God. Jesus lives in her'. Long association has in no way lessened but only confirmed this opinion. I have no hesitation in calling Claire a mystic, but then her way of prayer is extraordinary, as I shall explain later. I call it 'light on' prayer.

It was Claire who drew my attention to Petra. I had known her for many years and certainly she was a faithful nun but there was nothing to single her out. In some ways others seemed more generous and sacrificial. She did nothing more than what others were doing. Claire told me quite emphatically that Petra was a mystic. I asked her why she said that. What did she see in Petra? 'Petra never says "no" to God, is always looking to him to see what he wants and, chief of all, accepts to be totally poor, to have no holiness of her own'. Oh, what an answer to my search this was! If this ordinary woman, who like me had never known spiritual experiences, who was always in darkness and aridity, was a true mystic just as Claire was, then mysticism had nothing to do with 'experiences'. What was mysticism? Surely Jesus living in one, self drained away. I began to question Petra and she admitted simply that she knew Claire was right. She was aware, in a way that she could not explain, that she was closely united to God, that she no longer lived by her own life. And so I thought and thought, mercilessly tapping both Claire and Petra, and gradually things fell into place and I realised I had learnt something of immense importance that I must share with others. Claire and Petra are eager that I should write, and have fed me with ideas. This book is of three-fold authorship; hardly that, I am little more than the pen. I have looked with special interest at

St Thérèse of Lisieux, filled as she was with God's wisdom, who had the courage to affirm that God had done in her what St John of the Cross writes about in his *Canticle* and *Living Flame*, but in darkness and 'non-experience'.

The heart of mysticism is Jesus. Every age, I think, has its own understanding of Jesus, and this appears in its art, literature, the simple devotions of the people and in the way the mystical life is experienced and expressed. I don't know much about it though it interests me. I happen to be Mistress of Novices and so have contact with young people and the modern mind. My keenest interest lies in trying to discern what the Holy Spirit is showing us of Jesus today, for this understanding of him in whatever age, though it can be attributed to all sorts of natural factors, ultimately derives, in so far as it is truth, from the Spirit of Truth. Is it possible to say what particular aspect of the incarnation is holding men's hearts today and shaping their lives, or rather, what aspect God wills should hold their hearts and shape their lives? I would venture that it is precisely that of Christ crucified in weakness, the wisdom and the power of God; the revelation of God in the face of Christ Jesus delivered up to weakness and to death. This is the mystery of God, who is no benevolent almighty, lavishing gifts upon his creatures from afar, but love seeking intimacy, love that does not shout in the market place but whispers in the heart; love that is vulnerable, delivered into our hands to dispose of as we choose.

I have at least three reasons for thinking this. One is that man, today as never before, it seems, thinks he can do without God; at any rate he does not need him as an explanation. Mysteries which formerly pointed to the divine have been uncovered, their earthly roots laid bare; the frontiers of the supernatural have receded so far that for many they are no longer there. Need we lament this? I think not. It is a blessing that God wills; here is the opportunity for spiritual growing up. It means God has nothing to commend himself to us but his own self, and who does not want to be accepted for what he really is? But how vulnerable, how defenceless this makes him; only love will take him in. This insight into the helplessness of God, far from ending in sentimental devotionalism, means a testing of faith to the utmost, a veritable ordeal by fire.

Then there is the paradox that, in spite of man's awareness of his dazzling powers, he is overwhelmed with a sense of helplessness. His growing mastery over nature ends by making him its pitiful victim. We are afraid; more and more we realise that the world in which we live is being controlled by forces seemingly outside ourselves, leaving us to stand by helpless. We are prisoners of our limitations. There is no escape; the demons chaining us are every bit as real as those our naive forefathers feared. Who can save us? Only God who, to free us from these demons, came to us in our own condition; he shares our fate to deliver us from it.

Here biblical exegesis plays into our desperate hands, highlighting as it does the true humanity of the Lord. No matter how lively our faith was in the past it seems we could not break away from the notion that somehow Jesus was protected by his divinity; that he was not helpless as we are. We did not take literally 'a man like us in all things but sin'. Now we grasp that in fact he was wholly unprotected; that he experienced to the depths what it means to be a man, an unprivileged, helpless man who could be put away without any consequences—a man like us in all things.

To acknowledge that in our present age we have given the resurrection its true central place in our theology and, please God, in our lives, in no way contradicts what I have been saying. I think a wrong idea is around that stressing the resurrection means by-passing a great deal of human suffering, much that, in the cold light of day, brings us face to face with the pettiness, the sickening pettiness and futility of our human lot, the sordid pettiness of our own being, a suffering utterly lacking in nobility, grandeur. This is false. Jesus delivered us from suffering in the sense that he has given it meaning, not in the sense that it is no longer there. Dying will feel like dying and yet it won't be real dying, because Jesus has destroyed death. So suffering feels like suffering and nothing else. To live the risen life of Jesus is to accept the human lot in all its bitterness as he did, and surrender to the Father in it and through it. It does not mean trying to live in a state of emotional elation which takes the edge off human suffering.

Now if what I am saying is true we can expect a wonderful flowering of the mystical life in the measure that the conditions already present are understood and exploited. For what is the mystical life but God coming to do what we cannot do; God touching the depths of being where man is reduced to his basic element? The mystical life is beyond our power, nothing we can do can bring us to it, but God is longing to give it to us, to all of us, not to a select few. He made us for this, to share his divinity, to become his sons and daughters in very truth, with all that this implies. The prerequisite on our part is an acceptance of poverty, of need, of helplessness; the deep awareness that we need Jesus our saviour who alone brings God and man together, who is our holiness.

Hence I want to insist that this book is meant for all. If I indulge in technical terms such as 'purgative state' or 'dark night', it is only so that those familiar with these notions may be helped to understand what they mean. Those unfamiliar with them need not bother about them. It is not the terms but the substance that matters.

Again, if I seem to be confining my observations, examples, instances, to the very narrow circle of the religious life, mostly indeed the enclosed life, this is simply because that is the only environment of which I have living knowledge. This too is why I sometimes speak of 'she' without of course meaning to restrict my words to one sex rather than another. I feel it would be presumptuous of me to talk about situations and ways of life of which I have no practical experience. But how different this is from saying that I am not at one with men and women at large, understanding them at the only level that matters: their needs, aspirations, fears, bewilderments. Above all, understanding to some extent the immensity of God's love for each one of us and his overwhelming longing to draw us to himself and bring us to that fulfilment for which he made us.

To each one I would cry: 'Wake up! wake up out of your world of illusions. Look at God. There are no limits to what he will do for you if only you will trust him utterly'. You may find some of this book discouraging, but that can only be because, so to speak, you are standing on the wrong foot; are, in fact, still in your illusion even though you may think you are far advanced. If this book is saying anything it is this: none of us has any grounds for hope and confidence but the sheer goodness of God, the God,who never disappoints. Discouragement can only arise when I am thinking that it is what *I* do that is most important. No doubt God makes demands on us; all love does, but he alone can enable us to fulfil these demands. All he asks is that we trust him, take him at his word and do what we can and then we shall find that, in him, we can do what we can't. 'It is confidence and confidence alone that leads to love'. We can't love God; we can only want to love him and even that 'want' is his blessed gift. It is the same whether we are just starting out — we must take God at his word, do what we can to please him, go on trusting, never asking for proofs: or whether we think we are far along the road and then are faced with the shattering fact (in itself too painful to take) that we have scarcely set out — we must cast ourselves into his arms, drop the sense of our own achievement, count it as 'refuse for the sake of Christ' and in that act we have leapt along the road further than we can know.

'Children, how hard it is for those who trust in riches to enter the kingdom of God . . . And they were exceedingly astonished, and said to him: Then who can be saved? Jesus looked at them and said: With men it is impossible, but not with God; for all things are possible with God' (Mk 10:24 — 27). O Jesus, look at us, at each one of us, with that look which sees us as we are in our cowardice, in our complacency; with that look so full of love which shows us to ourselves, and in that look may we understand your words and live by them, casting aside our foolish 'riches', that God may be good to us to his heart's content.

1

LOOKING AFRESH

Yes, this is what we must do, look with fresh eyes at unchange-
able truth, extracting it from the formulations and wrappings
of earlier times. We want this truth to be living for us. Not a
few of the conclusions we draw—Claire, Petra and myself
insofar as I understand these things—may sound strange, even
revolutionary, but the thoughtful reader should recognise that
the strangeness is due to the fact that we are looking at truth
through the lens of modern insights. The basic truth which
this book is all about is that God, in his love, offers himself to
us as our fulfilment and perfect happiness. He chooses to draw
us into his own radiant life. He calls us to transcend our
natural limitations. This call, his gracious working in us
beyond our natural limits and operations, and the transcen-
dent goal to be reached, are precisely what we call the mystical.
It is the old, familiar doctrine of sanctifying grace and the
divine indwelling.

There are two partners in this dialogue of love, God and
man, and both our understanding of God and our understanding of man will affect the way in which we think of and
try to express the mystical. A great, important insight of our
times is that of man becoming. Earlier generations conceived
of the world and man as static. Man was there waiting to be
explored. If he was fortunate enough to be baptised and had

not separated himself from God by sin, then he could be sure
he was in a state of sanctifying grace and that God dwelt within
him. Think of your soul as a castle, St Teresa tells us, God
dwells in the innermost room. You, as yet, do not and you
must learn to go within, from room to room until you reach
the innermost centre where he is. The rooms are there, it is just
that you haven't learned to enter them. But nowadays we see
things differently. The rooms are *not* there! We grasp that we
are gradually coming into being; the potentiality which we
are — unique in each instance — is slowly 'realised'. How can
God dwell in depths that are not there as yet? We are much
more conscious than our predecessors that we *are* body, not an
'I' possessing a soul and a body. I am soul, I am body; and not
more soul than body. What is more, I can have absolutely no
knowledge save what comes to me through the body. There is
no other way into the self. How incredibly limiting when I
think of knowing and loving the infinite God! God alone can
touch my spirit directly, transcending these limitations and
this is what we mean by his mystical activity.

We are eager to stress that the mystical is of the essence of
christianity, not the privileged way of the few. To be more
precise: it means being wholly possessed by God and that is
holiness. One cannot be holy unless one is a mystic and if we do
not become mystics in this life we become such hereafter. This
is the same thing as saying that we cannot come to God by our
own steam, he alone can bring us to himself. Now the vast
majority of spiritual authors, St Teresa among them, claim
that there are two paths to holiness, the mystical way and the
ordinary way. This we cannot accept. The notion of the dual
carriage-way derives from a misconception which another
modern insight has led us to correct. The mystical has been
identified with certain experiences. When these are present in
a person such a one is a mystic or contemplative; he or she has

received the gift of infused contemplation, not essential for holiness but undoubtedly a great help towards it. Inevitably you get overtones of a high road and a low road.

Almost at random I quote a writer typical of this view: 'An exact notion of what the mystical life really is . . . it is the sensation which the soul feels of God's presence within it, a sort of feeling of God in the soul's centre' (cf Lejeune: *Introduction to the Mystical Life*). He quotes a range of authors to support his assertion — Gerson, St Teresa, Lallement, Surin, Courbon, Poulain. Firmly we deny the identification of this experience with the mystical grace of God. This 'sensation' *may* be flowing into the psyche from God's touch on the spirit but it may equally have another source. Not only is this 'sensation' or similar experience not the mystical grace but is not even a criterion of its presence. Our knowledge of psychology has made us healthily sceptical of much of what was formerly thought to be supernatural. I want to make a careful distinction between what is happening and what is thought to be known of this happening. 'Thought to be' — the reservation is deliberate, for the mystical happening, normally, cannot be known. True there are effects, but the only reliable one is growing selflessness.

St Teresa indeed insists that the way we live is the only criterion of the genuineness of prayer, and yet she is not wholly convincing because of her practical preoccupation with 'favours'. She claims, and many others with her, that a more intense emotional *experience* of prayer means a more advanced *state* of prayer: it is thus she distinguishes the prayer of quiet and that of union. We think this evaluation false, based as it is on an intensity which is physical. What would have happened if Teresa and John of the Cross had had our knowledge of the unconscious? Surely they would have interpreted their experiences differently. We know that drugs can produce identical states of awareness, so can extreme fasting and techniques of Yoga. Take St Teresa's understanding of 'locutions'. For her, they simply must come from God or from the devil, there is no possible alternative. True, she allows for the self talking to the self but then, she says, these are not locutions, and it is only the simpleton with an over-vivid imagination who would go in for that sort of thing. It could not have occurred to her that the mysterious unconscious might be the source of them all. No, we insist again, progress means responding more and more to God quite regardless of what we experience or don't experience at prayer.

The mystical life is rooted in Jesus, 'no one comes to the Father except by me'. He is our holiness and he alone. We have only to look at his life to be sure that holiness in this life will be without grandeur, beset with weakness. This marks it off absolutely from Eastern pagan mysticism and all forms of so-called 'natural mysticism', the keynote of which is 'exaltation', a being lifted out of the searing drabness of human life. We cannot say that christian mystics have ignored this aspect. Who could say it of St Teresa with her passionate love of our Lord? But possibly they were incapable of appreciating as we do the reality of his humanity, 'a man like us. . . .' For Teresa he is always 'His Majesty' and this, I feel sure, influenced her interpretation of what was happening to her. Exterior trials could be integrated easily, but interior annihilation, weakness . . . not just at a stage of the journey but all along the way and at its end, at the stage of transforming union itself? One senses an uneasiness when, in her seventh mansion, chapter 4, she admits that those in this sublime state are occasionally left to the 'weakness of their nature'. 'The venomous creatures from the moat around the castle and the other mansions at once unite to revenge themselves for the time when they were deprived of their power'. She adds 'this lasts but a short time . . . this trouble rarely happens'; its purpose is our Lord's wish to keep the soul humble. A rather strange explanation when all is said and done. It is worth having a look at a letter she wrote to Gratian in the last year of her life (1 Sept. 1582). She expresses her loneliness and hurt at his leaving her when she felt she needed him. 'Your frequent letters to me do not suffice to alleviate my distress . . . so keenly did I feel your being away at such a time that I lost the desire to write to you.' Would it have occurred to her that her wounded feelings, as well as the troubles and temptations she refers to, were an aspect of the state of union, not a sort of interlude during which she was deprived of the divine companion? Could she have seen them as the *result* of the union, of Jesus living in her the human condition?

We take over the almost unanimous tradition that in the spiritual life there are basically three stages although these can be subdivided: the purgative, illuminative, unitive stages, to use the common terms. We differ from most authors, at least in emphasis, by insisting that these three stages are totally distinct from one another, each representing a wholly new relation to God or a wholly new intervention on the part of God. The view that they are not so distinct but merge into one another is again based, it seems, on emotional experience. Thus a person may know a period of seeming illumination followed by one of dryness and darkness, and again by an experience of joy and light perhaps greater than the first. Apparently the soul is going back and forth from the illuminative to the purgative. The interpretation does not seem valid to us.

This chapter has the nature of an overture. The themes introduced are to be played out in the following pages. But at the outset we sought for an image to clarify our thoughts as others have done before us: a castle of many mansions, a ladder with its successive steps . . . Claire devised the image of three islands, and the more I think about it the more satisfactory it seems. It helps to show the three stages and their relation to and distinctness from each other. We have to imagine that we are looking down on to a vast sea in which are set three islands. They really are islands, that is they are cut off from one another, for there are no harbours, no boats, no traffic between them. Those who live on the first island feel it is the whole world, they do not know there is anything beyond. Those on the second may know there is an island they have left but they do not know there is a third as well. From our vantage point we see that there is a narrow bridge spanning the sea between the first island and the second. It is not as if you have just to make for that bridge and go over it; you cannot know it is there, still less can you come to it by yourself. You have to be brought to it. It is the only way to the second island and it represents the beginnings of mystical prayer, what John of the Cross calls the passive night of sense. Even from our vantage point we can see no bridge between the second and the third island. How a person passes from the one to the other we do not know. This is the result of a divine intervention in the most absolute sense, it is shrouded in mystery. But now let us look at the first of the islands.

2

THE FIRST ISLAND

Every man is in dialogue with God. The saint says 'yes' to him, the sinner, 'no'. As for the rest of us, it is a medley of tones and semi-tones, minor and major thirds of 'noes' and 'yesses'. To put it in another way, the sun shines on all. The very few stand fully exposed to the light and heat—others shrink away into dark corners where it cannot penetrate. The rest in varying degrees shelter or hide from its radiance. But the sun goes on shining and God goes on loving us, trying to prepare us to receive him, drawing us to himself.

What a vast land is this first island and how densely populated! It can be presumed that the great majority of men and women dwell on it. Its inhabitants range from those with the crudest of moralities, following their feebly-lit, maybe erroneous conscience, to those who like the young man in the gospel, can sincerely say of the commandments of God, 'all these have I kept from my youth'. But God doesn't want us to stay here; he didn't create, didn't redeem us for this. Much of what is said in this book would be cruel if somehow we were meant to stay on the first island or could not move off it. We *can* move off it. Oh, not of our own ability, only God can enable us to transcend its bounds, but he is all eagerness to do so and this book aims to show how he works and how we must respond.

Of course, we must allow for the possibility of sinners, believers or unbelievers, for those who have deliberately chosen to dwell in the caverns underground, but how easily we can be mistaken in pointing to them. The more I have looked at the world of men, read history, novels, case-histories of crime, the more convinced I am that man is not wicked but blind. Often you get the impression that mankind is wandering blindly and aimlessly in a great, dark forest, getting entangled, falling into pits, with no sense of direction; not wicked but blind and helpless. God has given some of us lanterns to bear in this dark forest, lighting up the path for others. We are endowed with the mental and psychic health denied to many, a good background, education, let alone spiritual insight, and it is we who are more likely to be sinners.

As I said, if I confine my references and instances to religious life, it is simply because this is the situation of which I have living knowledge, not because what I am writing about concerns religious only. Far from it; others can make their own application. My worry when I allow my mind to consider sinners would be the slack religious, the one who has been given a lamp which she has allowed to go out. There may be nothing outrageous, just a persistent choosing of self in small ways, shown by grumbling, discontent, the attitude which judges everything by whether I *like* it: horarium, office, community functions, human contacts, food; if any do not please, if they disturb or inconvenience, then there are complaints, either externally or within, according to temperament. There is a bitterness which is an infallible indication of selfishness. One must question whether such a one is in a state of grace. Can one continually choose self even though the occasions be small and still be in a state of friendship with God? Isn't this to choose dwelling in the underground caverns?

Now certain questions about our relationship to God, on this island as on the others, need to be asked. First, precisely what it is. Next, what do we experience of it? Finally, what is our response? On this island the way we relate to God is still our own. This is what distinguishes it from the other two. God always offers himself to us — 'see, I stand at the door and knock' — but as yet we cannot respond and give ourselves to him. Though the heritage is ours we cannot use it, as a baby inheriting great estates cannot enjoy them until many years later when they become really his.

Here on this island then the loving action of God is limited to enabling us to accept revealed truth and at this stage faith does no more than make acceptance possible, it does not substitute for what we can and must do ourself; it is more or less notional and not part of the self. It is truth about God, God 'out there'. We do not know God himself and therefore do not love and choose him as such. All we see are traces of God and what we choose are created realities — concepts, ideas. Until God intervenes mystically, that is until he creates his own secret route into the self, we can go no further. We can only peer with half-blind eyes into the mist-bound terrain, looking for the footprints of God and making tiny, shuffling movements in his direction. That is, the self knows and loves in the way proper to it and this is inexpressibly limited, and so can never know and love God in himself unless God intervenes and transcends this ordinary mode.

Over the surface of this island is a honeycomb of caves leading to the dark caverns which lie under the whole expanse of the land. At any time we may turn aside, drawn by their secret allure, and descend into the dark. A sweet, fascinating, deadly charm lies therein, that of independence, 'godhead', the primal, ever-recurring temptation. Up above by contrast there is a law to be obeyed even though it is so attuned to us as not to be imposed from without but rises up from within, our own truth and glory.

Mist-bound terrain, I have called it. There is a paradox here. This island does not seem mist-bound to its inhabitant. Quite the contrary. It is beautiful, abounding in lovely things. Just because we are limited to our own activity, just because God is giving himself only in a far-off sort of way under ideas and concepts which are the proper data of human activity, we are at peace. We can cope, are in control of the situation. Often enough, we will feel spiritually capable, will feel that we really do know and love God.

A person on this island can be likened to primitive man in the world. It took him thousands of years before he could tame the beasts, sail on the water . . . not so much because he could not, as because he never dreamed such things were possible. The sense of well-being on this island must be stressed. This island is our natural habitat and we feel in control as we want to be. But if God is to take possession of us we must be drawn out of this security, we must lose control, or rather hand over the control of our life to God. We must leave our country and our father's house. Immediately, surely, we glimpse something of the choice that is to face us. Will we allow God to draw us away or will we persist in staying where we are on our own beautiful island?

Recently I was asked to read a book which vividly illustrated this point for me. It happened to be on yoga but in many ways its teaching corresponds with commonly accepted notions of the spiritual life. It revealed in a startling way the cleavage between it and christian mysticism, and also the enormous difficulties it creates for God. There is no question of my discussing yoga in itself. It would be sheer presumption as I do not know enough about it. My concern is only with that search for what is thought to be the mystical experience or awareness. It is quite clear that what is sought is what man can achieve

with no transcendence of his nature. The yogist, so the book
claims, strives by self-discipline and especially by an effort to
empty the mind, to free the psyche for an experience of the
self. All along it is a question of making oneself perfect,
becoming the perfect man, removed from the weaknesses and
wearinesses of human life. This is a most subtle form of pride
and a most effective block to God's love. Christian mysticism is
essentially God's work, and progressively the soul must abandon its own striving, abandon even its desire for perfection,
which in biblical terms is the law. Incidentally, another point
of cleavage with the christian tradition is the emphasis on
mind, the emptying of the mind. It seems all the energy of the
soul is employed in emptying the mind. Is there any left to love
with?

I fear many a sincere person is seeking an 'experience', an
exalted state of consciousness. But this 'experience' is not God.
God is surely knocking on his heart but can he hear him? God's
mystical intervention would mean the collapse of that proud
human structure. Gone the fine control of the mind, gone the
sense of being a very special person, a superman, a spiritual
man. Is it likely that one who has attained this magnificent
goal is likely to make the right choice? This is rather an
extreme case but it highlights the choice that faces everyone
living a serious spiritual life. God wants to intervene. Will we
let him? Everything depends on the answer. Yet how much
serious direction has been and still is geared, in reality, not to
seeking God's will in order to surrender to him in fulfilling it,
but to self-perfection, self-glorification. The whole work of this
island is to do God's will, that is, fulfil the law. Man is always
tempted when doing the works of the law to live by the law,
whereas the true disciple of Christ lives by the Spirit. He
cannot live by the Spirit unless he keeps the law; the Spirit will
drive him to an ever more perfect fulfilling of the law. But the

deadly temptation of this island is to live by the law and make it alone our security.

However, the danger is double-edged and there seems equal fear nowadays of a non-fulfilling of the law in favour of living by the Spirit. Freedom, responsibility, maturity—these concepts can be greatly misapplied. I question whether we religious are being serious enough in our education. We lay on plenty of theology, biblical exegesis, psychology, involvement in the active apostolate, but what about the spiritual life itself, without which all the rest is valueless or nearly so?

Young people come to us precisely for that spiritual formation, for the support we can give them. Rare is the person who can 'go it alone', who has the tenacity, the sheer hunger for this, and it is awareness of weakness that brings an aspirant to a community. When one thinks that St Teresa waits until her fifth mansion, our second island, before allowing freedom, before trusting us in dangerous situations, knowing that then God holds us closely and our love is strong enough to stand firm, it seems naive, to say the least, to leave our young people to fend for themselves, to make decisions in areas where they have almost no light as yet. It is a fact of human life that the majority of people, given strong enlightened leadership and the support of a proper environment, can live a good, meaningful life, but without these helps they flounder. Religious are no exception. The majority need good leadership and some structure. To think otherwise is to be unrealistic. It is within this framework that they can be helped to grow to maturity. No one denies that there was too much support, too much control and domination in the past; it is a happy mean we need.

In order to treat of human life on this island I confine myself to two groups of inhabitants. Both are likely to read this book, both are consciously living an interior life. One group comprises those for whom this island is their proper place, a stage of their journey—they are on their way across it—rather as childhood is a state proper to the child but one which must be outg vn. The other consists of those who have chosen to live on this island, have made it their base when God would have led them further. This situation is no less incongruous than that of an adolescent or adult who refuses to grow up but persists in living like a child. The whole of the fifth chapter will be concerned with them.

For convenience sake, I will call the first group 'beginners'. When one approaches the vast subject of training, guiding, counselling one feels bewildered. A whole book would not suffice for all that should be said. I must limit myself. A few fundamentals must be dealt with.

To get a unifying orientation we must look steadily at the end. What is the end? Nothing less than total possession by God. Progress then will mean, not a building up of the human ego, not an acquiring of 'perfection', but a growing surrender to God, allowing him to control life more and more.

'The cross is little understood today' a spiritual person remarked sadly. Has it ever been understood? In the past you got a stress on suffering which perverted christianity into 'crosstianity', the idea that you are only pleasing God when you are suffering and the more suffering the better. All sorts of errors lie behind this attitude and what a blasphemous caricature of our God! Fear and hatred of matter—one becomes spiritual the more one is removed from matter and this means from the body and the emotions—which is utterly unchristian because inhuman; together with the notion that we were redeemed by suffering, that since Christ suffered we must suffer too. Push this to its logical conclusion and you cannot have too much suffering. But it is false. It was love that redeemed us, love that did the Father's will no matter what the cost, love that was total surrender. It was through suffering but it was not the suffering itself that brought us to the Father. It is because suffering is a fact in human life from which there is no escape that Christ suffered. He suffered because we must suffer. He accepted our human lot and transformed it into the path to glory.

And yet we do seem to be going to the opposite extreme. Obligations no longer bind if they involve suffering, if there is strain or difficulty. People walk out of a marriage, out of religious life, out of the priesthood, because there is an apparent lack of fulfilment; life is felt to impose a burden which we are free to throw off. Accepting the will of God at whatever cost, certain that he gives us strength whatever we feel, this is to follow Jesus and be his disciple. One feels there is a great deal of frivolity nowadays, a lack of seriousness in the face of life. Yet think of the gravity of our life-span, how much is at stake. We have only one life to live. It is easy to think we are doing God a favour, that there is an alternative to total commitment. Is there? What is it?

As to the austerity we impose upon ourselves it can be looked upon in various ways. The obvious one today that no christian can ignore is that of going without that others may have; a practical application at a personal level of the truth that the world's resources are not the monopoly of the few. It seems to me this must affect us all in regard to food, clothing, heating, water, etc. It means 'no' to many extra comforts we had come to take for granted.

For St Teresa austerity is the path to freedom, which makes sense. In an enclosed life it has perhaps even greater significance. Just because on the human level it is rather a dull life with little stimulus and diversion, it is easy to get occupied with ourselves and our bodily needs and it requires resolution to guard against this. But I see that the deeper significance of a self-imposed austerity, after that of justice and charity, is the practical affirmation that God is my life and I will let nothing take the edge off the need for him. It is a way of living out our hunger and thirst and refusing to be satisfied. Only one way, it is true, but we are body and express our hearts through our bodies and it seems inconsistent to keep on telling God he is my all, I want nothing but him, and then living as if I had settled for this world with plenty of all I need around me. We need to feel that we are in exile. Were we to have the tiniest glimpse of God, we would lose desire for anything else. Should not a loyal love maintain this attitude even in darkness, when there is no glimpse given? Then it is hard to maintain austerity and refuse to fall back on little comforts that take the edge off the feeling of need and emptiness. However, this must not be carried too far. My general policy is that when I can bear a bit of cold, fatigue and so on without preoccupation then I do, but if it gets me down and becomes a 'thing' then I alleviate it if I am free to do so. If I am not, if duty is involved or the well-being of another, then I must put up with the hardship and be pre-occupied! But I cannot think of our Lord being terribly interested in whether we have a bit more or less of this and that in itself.

We have to learn to take our hands off the controls of our lives in the exercise of obedience. In our context this means an intelligent submission to people and events; the acceptance of that discipline in our lives, that curtailing of self-determination which belongs to our human lot and against which we jib. It is to recognise God's hand in all that befalls us, recognising his will mediated to us and surrendering to it. Both St Teresa and St John labour the ascetical benefits of community life whether in the narrow or broad sense. We love God in loving others. We expose ourselves to God in exposing ourselves to others. The full acceptance of obedience and refusal to evade; the full acceptance of community living and refusal to evade; the full

acceptance of the duties of our state of life and refusal to
evade, these are the highways to God. We cannot stress this too
much. I am always impressed by St John's 'Precautions'. Here
he is out to counsel contemplatives how to surrender themselves to God, how to expose themselves to his mystical action,
and all the stress is on community life.

'Freedom' is indeed a key word but how little understood. I
am reminded here of Ursula le Guin's beautiful story *The
Tombs of Atuan*. Tenar from tiniest childhood has been
brought up in the dark world of the Tombs as its high-priestess,
Arha; she knows no other home. She gets her first glimpse of
light and the world beyond in the person of the young mage
Ged who dares to trespass into her dark domain to search for
the lost half of the Ring of Eirreth-Akbe, the key to peace. He is
at her mercy, but what he is, his freedom, wholeness, trans-
parency and his trust allure her. They awaken in her longings
she cannot understand, and a disgust for her own dark world.
But the struggle is great; in the dark world she is sole mistress,
here she is at home; this is the world she knows, in which she
tastes the sweet charm of power and independence.

'I don't know what to do. I am afraid' . . . 'I am afraid of
the dark'.

He answered softly. 'You must make a choice. Either you
must leave me, lock the door, go up to your altars and give
me to your Masters . . . and that is the end of the story—or,
you must unlock the door, and go out of it, with me . . .
And that is the beginning of the story. You must be Arha,
or you must be Tenar. You cannot be both' . . .

'If I leave the service of the Dark Ones, they will kill me. If
I leave this place I will die'.

'You will not die. Arha will die'.

'I cannot . . .'

'To be reborn one must die, Tenar. It is not so hard as it looks from the other side' . . .
'I will come with you', she said.

Each of us has to look into our dark world, recognise the forces that bind us, the blind instincts, the compulsions which, though they give the illusion of power, freedom, adulthood, ensnare us. We have to fight our way free; renounce the Dark Powers, learn to judge and act from our centre. Only then are we human and personal. This work of self-knowledge is absolutely essential. Happy are we if we have a Ged to trust and love us enough to enable us to break free. But all of us have the true Ged, Jesus, the one who has come down, a light into our darkness; come down to take us back with him to true freedom, life in his Father.

Once freed from the caves, Tenar knows a brief space of halcyon bliss with Ged on the mountain. She wants to stay there, but they must journey on. Then she begins to taste the bitterness of her self and her past, and the sheer weight of freedom. There comes a time when face to face with its implications she is even tempted to kill Ged, her liberator.

Eventually they put out to sea.

'Now', he said, 'now we're away, now we're clear, we're clean gone, Tenar. Do you feel it?'
She did feel it. A dark hand had let go its lifelong hold upon her heart. But she did not feel joy, as she had in the mountains. She put her head down in her arms and cried, and her cheeks were salt and wet. She cried for the wasted years in bondage to a useless evil. She wept in pain because she was free.

What she had begun to learn was the weight of liberty. Freedom is a heavy load, a great and strange burden for the spirit to undertake. It is not easy. It is not a gift given, but a choice made, and the choice may be a hard one. The road goes upward towards the light, but the laden traveller may never reach the end of it.

Ged let her cry and said no word of comfort.

How many of us are prepared to accept our destiny and live it out whatever the cost? The soul is now about to face a momentous choice. God is coming to take her into freedom. Will she accept? Will she pay the price?

3

THE BRIDGE

By 'the bridge' is meant the occasional mystical intervention of
God which, responded to, fits the soul to reach and live on the
second island; it can be identified with what St John of the
Cross calls the passive night of sense. Must there be a bridge?
We are quite certain that there must be a first island and that
everyone, except our Lord and our Lady, is born into it, comes
to birth in the caverns under its surface. But is the bridge a
necessity or can it be dispensed with? Everything is possible to
God. He could, if he chose to do so, take a person straight from
the first island to the second. But would such powerful
intervention be too devastating, especially for a young child? It
seems that occasionally you do meet a person who has never
lived on the first island for any length of time. As soon as they
were capable of choice, the mystic life began. The bridge? The
second island? I do not know. Certainly the second island in
the teens. This seems very exceptional and the normal pattern
is of a considerable time living on the first island, a long time
on the bridge and, for those who get there, a long time on the
second island.

Why does it happen that God occasionally gives to a young
child or adolescent powerful graces which for others he reserves
until later life or perhaps withholds? We do not know. Human
response comes in somewhere, but is not the capacity to res-

pond, especially in a yet unproven young child, itself a gift?
Although to an outsider there might seem to have been
generous self-giving, the recipient knows that it is not so. It has
been gift all along the way. 'You have received without pay'
(Mt 10:8). I am sure the gift is not meant only for the recipient.
In some way it is given for others. Too easily when we speak of
such things we get the impression that others, the 'mere rank
and file', are less loved, less cared for by God. This is not so
and near blasphemy. Every soul is loved uniquely; 'as though
she were the only one in creation' is the conviction of those with
insight. The divine thought, the divine love and tender,
watchful providence embraces each one uniquely, and all that
has happened or will happen is for that one uniquely. Baffling
to our limited imagination, but the truth. On this sure rock of
God's love we must build our lives. From the outset, every
effort must be made to convince ourselves of this love and to
deepen our faith in it: God's unfailing, unshakable love for
me, no matter what it feels like, no matter how unlike love it
seems. What can matter in this life save to surrender to this
love?

Because God loves us and longs to give himself to us, to be
our joy, we can count on his doing so, and what we are looking
at now is a very intimate encounter between God and the one
he loves. Before I say more about it I want to say a little about
the importance of giving time to prayer. God can give himself
at any time, be it during the time of prayer or during activity.
But he is most likely to visit us in this special way during prayer
because only then are we likely to let him in and our deep self
respond to his visit. Prayerful activity can be no substitute for
time set aside exclusively for God. How sad it is that prayer in
this sense is not part and parcel of the normal christian life,
and yet without it one cannot be fully christian. People do not
understand this and who is to tell them? An earlier generation

had the rosary; a brief space was reserved for God and this gave him his chance. What of today? If only catholics were taught to avail themselves fully of their assistance at mass, the reception of the sacrament of penance, their morning and night prayers; taught that God is longing to draw near to them to work in them; taught how they must hold themselves attentive before him, not expecting 'something to happen' — that sort of thing has nothing to do with prayer — but believing that he is working in them. It is moving to see how in old age a habit of prayer, formed in the demanding busy years, bears rich fruit — simply, unselfconsciously.

The sacraments are direct encounters with God in Christ. In them God touches us directly, he himself, unmediated. This is the mystical life in its concentrated form, flashing out in all its intolerable brightness for one vitalising minute. But we can only take this brightness in the measure we are there for it. Conversely, the more we expose what we are, however small that may be, the more there becomes of us. It can only be in utter mystery. What happens at communion? Confession? No human mind can comprehend the encounter because it is of its essence too personally God.

Speaking of prayer, I am reminded of Petra's reaction to a group of young people who were talking about prayer. 'That isn't prayer', she cried, 'that detached attitude . . . prayer is falling on our Lord as a famished man falls on food, as a parched man gulps down water; is clinging to him as a drowning man to a spar . . . no detachment there! How to get them to see that they *need* him, can't *live* without him . . .?' Well, that is the point, a dweller on the first island cannot realise his need, cannot realise that he is blind, poor, sick. In a distant sort of way he knows these things because they are part of his faith, but he does not know them in a living way. They are not written in his flesh. When God draws near he will know them.

'You speak so much of the pain of experienced poverty but must it always be painful? Can it not be a joyful thing when one is certain of God's love, that he loves us in our poverty?' This heartfelt question from a sincere young person was answered by Claire in a parable.

High in the mountains of Africa lived a very primitive tribe. The world outside their own was the occasional glimpse of a jet streaking far over their heads, and this they thought was the gods throwing spears at one another. But one day, a white man appeared on the mountain, a young anthropologist, come to study them at close quarters, if they would have him. He was lodged in the chief's hut, lived there for some years, and fell in love with the chief's daughter. Up to then the girl had thought herself wealthy — was not her father the most powerful of their people? But the closer she grew to her white lover, the more she saw that her very riches — the family cattle, some pots and skins — were poverty compared to the possessions of her lover. He had stuffs and leathers and machines, steel to cut with and matches to make fire with and delicacies unimaginable. But she saw too that his greatest delight was to share his riches with her. Her lack merely aroused his bounty, so she knew her poverty primarily as a sweet thing, the occasion of giving pleasure to them both.

But that was only the beginning. A husband takes his wife to his own environment. The little African girl found it terrifyingly alien and now her grief began. For she found that her husband's enemies laughed behind his back at his primitive woman, and his friends pitied him. She had the bitter knowledge that she brought some sort of disgrace on her dear one. This was only the beginning of her sorrow. Her husband truly loved her, he longed to share his heart with her and take her completely into his life. But when he tried to speak of the things closest to him, she would hear his beloved voice falter, as she failed to follow even the meaning of the words, let alone the scope of his concepts. She was shut off from him by her poverty — and that gave him a wife in the physical sense only. He suffered from her inability and ignorances, and that to her was a distress almost beyond bearing.

And so we come to the third stage of poverty. The more she realised what her state meant to her lover, the more absolute became her will to escape from it, for his sake. Yet equally, the more clearly she saw that of herself there was no escape — it was a poverty too total to have within it any avenue to enrichment. But there was a third realisation that balanced the other two: that in her husband she had not only come to understand her poverty but in him she had infinite and ever-present redemption from it. If she was prepared to make cultural, personal, intellectual, spiritual growth the one overmastering preoccupation of her life, devote to it all her leisure, all her ingenuity, all her energies and never admit defeat — then from her husband she could receive all that his love had ready for her. So she set herself to work, learning, questioning, memorising, schooling herself to perceive and acquire all the elements of a foreign and highly sophisticated culture. She achieved her end. Elegant, witty, beautiful, between her and her husband there pass the intimate glances of complete spiritual understanding; she has an intuitive knowledge of how his mind works, having so closely conformed her own to it. Yet she has not lost anything at all of the natural woman he first fell in love with; on the contrary, she has only now become possessed of her own innate potentiality. Her enrichment has brought all that was there to flower. But now, more than ever, she knows it is all his doing. Every perception, every phase of growth came from his love and his teaching.

What happens? We cannot know, because this is a divine

work. God touches us directly without intermediaries or forms, by-passing the normal way in which the self encounters all that is not self. And for this brief moment of encounter we can say there is union. God unites himself to what is there, to as much of the self as is realised, but at this stage it is not much. Yet if we could see what was happening we would die of joy and wonder . . . that God should give himself thus to me! Nothing in creation bears comparison with it; it transcends all else. God unites himself to me and for the brief moment I love *him*, not an image of him, and this act of love too outstrips my ordinary operations. God shows himself—hence the name 'infused contemplation'. This knowledge is in the most secret self, not in the conscious mind.

It can never be emphasised enough, that mystical contemplation of itself cannot be experienced with the ordinary apparatus of experience: senses, conscious mind. God could switch on the light and then what is happening would be 'seen', but this rarely happens. Still, there will be effects and these will be observable though not for some time perhaps as, generally speaking, the touches of God at this stage are light and infrequent. We may not know anything of what has happened. It may be years before the grace is repeated.

To illustrate this we can think of our first island-dweller crossing the island on a well-worn, clear path. He can tread confidently for it is a path he understands. It has its difficulties and surprises but he can cope very well. After some time he begins to feel less sure, less steady on his feet, and then he realises that what was the path has become a sort of narrow causeway running over the land at an elevation—not high, he can easily get off. He did not notice when the change took place. Once he grasps the strangeness he is likely to jump off in fright onto the safe, sure earth. But now he finds there is no other path. He can go no further on the island; he can go round in circles, he can camp, but he can't progress: the only path of progress is that unpleasant bridge and so he is enticed to try it again. It won't feel any easier as he goes along, quite the contrary. It begins to span the sea—a narrow, slippery plank washed by the waves. He will be tempted to turn back to the security of the island he has left. He can do this at any time.

Translated into real life this means that we begin to feel bewildered, losing our taste for prayer and spiritual things. Our general state at prayer is one of confusion, darkness, boredom, helplessness; the very opposite in fact of what we expect progress to be like. This is the scandal, this is the crisis. Will we accept this disconcerting process and grow, or will we escape it, as we can to a great extent, preferring to live safely in the mist-bound first island in a state of blindness and feebleness which yet seem light and strength. This aridity may be very gradual and it may be some time before we notice it. The cause is obvious and has been noted already. Because God is showing *himself*, however dimly, the deep self loses its taste for what the mind can bring to it by way of ideas and concepts. The deep self has eaten of delicious food and now its palate is spoiled for what pleased it beforehand.

Another effect of this divine 'showing', which also will be very gradual, is a knowledge of self which becomes increasingly painful. It is characteristic of man to be blind and complacent and only God can deliver him from this condition. He has no idea how blind he is and is self-satisfied precisely because he lacks light and has no yard-stick for measuring progress. The light from this encounter with God reduces our self-image and this is extremely painful. Not only that, it makes demands upon us that we cannot meet. Hence a feeling of sinfulness and helplessness. We are being invited to cast off our illusions and stand in the truth. We hate this. We want to feel we are good, that we can control our lives. We do not want to admit that the good is beyond our reach. Of course we know in a notional way that it is, but when it comes to the crunch we do not know it; we want to 'do it ourselves', and when faced with this sense of 'everything going wrong', 'I can't pray', 'this isn't the spiritual life', 'I want God not this', we run away.

A third effect of the mystical grace is seen in the quality of life. This is hard to assess, and the older I get the more I realise that discernment of spirits is a gift and it is rare. All of us can estimate ordinary virtue, but when it comes to something more subtle than that, few can discern it. What I have in mind is an element, very diminutive perhaps, of that divine wisdom which baffles human wisdom, the folly of the cross. This is the most certain of all the signs of the mystical. There is a growing insight. We are beginning to see God where we never thought he was, in what upsets our preconceived ideas of God, of what he does and what his drawing near will be like. We shall begin to listen to God, to what he is asking here and now, and this may run counter to what we have been conditioned to expect. It may set us at odds with the milieu in which we live. The tendency to criticise others will disappear and our heart will become kind and compassionate. It won't just be a question of doing things for others, serving them — this need not go beyond the bounds of 'virtue', of 'the law' — but a true preferring of others to self in all things. In general there will be a growing willingness to accept on every level, a sense of unimportance, to become as small as a child. To draw near to God is to abandon every ambition, and when we have abandoned earthly ones we grasp at spiritual ones. The ego must begin to die. Only God's mystical action can bring this about. On the first island, no matter what our efforts, the ego remains obstinately enthroned, and the very effort to live a spiritual life, to be virtuous, strengthens its position.

In discussing the third effect of God's mystical grace I have already shown the direction in which we must move: to an acceptance of growing helplessness and poverty. There will be no abandonment of the practice of virtue, of the seeking for God's will, but this will begin to have a different quality and what is more will provide little or no satisfaction. The right hand will not know what the left is doing. No longer will I feel I am a faithful servant. On the contrary I will see that even my best works are tainted with pride. Then we must beware of escaping from this painful situation, jumping off the bridge back on to the first island or, if we are further on over the sea, slithering back to where the bridge runs overland and hence seems more secure.

We may try to hold on to or return to more naturally satisfying ways of prayer. This is a subtle point and needs expanding. Though God's intervention disorientates to a greater or lesser extent the natural activity of the soul, nevertheless the mind can usually continue to function and perhaps better than ever. We may be capable of writing or giving a brilliant conference, the fruit of reflection and meditation. Thus we could happily spend our prayer time with thoughts and the time would pass pleasantly. After all they are thoughts about God! But if we are under the influence of the mystical action of God our inmost heart will tell us that, for us, this sort of mental activity at prayer is a distraction and an infidelity. It is quite incapable of nourishing our being. It merely occupies us and gives an illusory sense that we have passed the time well, achieved something. God asks us to sacrifice this mental activity at prayer time. We are leaving him to think about him. We must do our best to remain in his presence, bearing patiently and trustfully the sense of futility, the boredom, the lack of satisfaction at having made prayer well.

However, we cannot take for granted that once God has

begun to intervene we can abandon ourselves to passivity. Whenever we are conscious that we are benefitting by reflections, that through them we are growing in power to choose God's will, we should use them. It would be presumption and foolish to induce a state of aridity because this indicates progress. Both Teresa and John warn us against this fruitless aridity.

We can fall into apathy, discouragement, and fail to correspond with God, continually bemoaning our state, whipping ourselves, indulging in self-pity, which is a covert way of getting at God. I dare not blame him so I blame myself and let off my resentment in this way. What God is asking of me now is to actuate my growing capacity to choose, and to use these difficulties as opportunities for choosing him unselfishly. I have to let go my poor, aching self, drop myself, move out into the darkness to the certainty of God's love for me, of his goodness and fidelity. I know God loves me and will never reject me; he embraces sinners. What do my feelings matter? I will be at rest and refuse to lose heart. I will go on lifting my heart to him, knocking at the door, seeking, all the while knowing that he is with me and loves me. All my feelings may scream against this but I do not trust anything in myself, only in God. I trust, not because I am good and therefore pleasing to him but because he is good and makes me pleasing to him by giving himself to me. Now is the time to carry into reality the words of trust I have uttered, words of praise of God's goodness. Now is the time to show God I mean them.

Both Teresa and John speak of being rejected by God — more, John says the soul believes it is abandoned by him. To feel abandoned is one thing, to believe it another and contrary to faith. God has told us emphatically that he never abandons his children, even in their sin. Our God is the God of sinners. We must simply reject this notion of John's, which does not square with the gospel and therefore is not authentic. We have to remember his dreadful experience in the prison of Toledo: solitary confinement, near starvation, lack of light and air, brain-washing. Was he able to distinguish between what was purely natural in his suffering—psychic anguish flowing from these cruel conditions—and what was the effect of God's touch? I think we have to bear this in mind when we consider what he says about the passive night of the spirit. I am afraid some people take hold of this idea of abandonment as the culminating spiritual trial and sure sign of great progress: they too think they are abandoned by God and oh, the sheer agony of it! This is nonsense and an insult to God. How much harm this play-acting does! How much depends on trying to be true, simple and single-minded, seeking God's good pleasure and not our own glory. To feel he doesn't care, isn't interested in me is very much part of mystic suffering, but I live by faith and not by what I feel. There is one suffering God *never* wishes us to bear, more, positively wills us never to bear—that of uncertainty regarding his love for us. Whatever other suffering he allows us to bear for our good, this he can never will. I know he loves me and I live by that certitude. To wallow in pseudo-suffering is to escape from the demands of living here and now, from giving God what he is asking here and now, which is undramatic, humdrum, mediocre, just what he asks of everyone else!

It is very easy to misunderstand St John of the Cross's teaching on the 'Nights'. It must be seen in the context of his times. We have to remember that all sorts of fantastic aberrations were masquerading as spirituality. There was a tremendous interest in 'experience', in feelings, visions and other phenomena. Likewise there was fanaticism. Spirituality was confused with frantic activities. John is crying out that people haven't a notion of what true spirituality is—it consists of none of these things but of complete denudation and surrender, a letting God work. He is telling them that they have no conception of the awful holiness of God and consequently of human dreadfulness. They imagine they can have God on the cheap. Just because they have unctuous feelings they think they are devout and loving, they feel they are truly spiritual people and encourage one another in their illusions.

John takes up his pen to shatter this play-play. He wants to show the bare bones of spirituality, the 'bare anatomy' which is not seen. He wants to show what contemplation really is and the awful price to be paid for God. And so he heavily underlines suffering and darkness. He was quite well aware of another side. He wrote two books on it, but there was no fear in his day of that being overlooked. It was his purpose to stress the pain and darkness, the deprivation; he writes a monograph on it and, highly emotional as he was, it assumes a dramatic, high-pitched intensity. But we must remember that this monograph is not the whole picture. Life even for one whose lot seems extremely hard, is never all darkness, pain and deprivation. Every life has at least its neutral periods if not its happy ones. It is important to get John in perspective. Failure to do so usually results in two false conclusions. Some people who see nothing in their lives resembling his nights tend to conclude, and perhaps others agree with them, that they have made no substantial progress. Worse, there are others who see pain and darkness as signs of deep spirituality. They suffer and that means that God must be working in them in a special way. They are God's chosen. Commonplace ups and downs, the lot of everyone, depression, moods, the wear and tear of life are blown up into a spiritual trial, a mystical ordeal.

The dark nights are by and large the common lot, the ordinary trials which everyone must undergo. These are precisely the means by which God purifies us: difficulties of temperament, ill-health, disappointments as well as the grievous sufferings of human beings, christian or no. We are back again at the old problem, the refusal to be human. We want to be big in our own eyes, in God's eyes and the eyes of others. And God wants us to be small, unimportant to ourselves, quite ordinary and commonplace. How wise he is, hiding his deepest action in what is utterly human. There is no pretext then for self-gratification; but we are incurable, we can find a pretext even here, casting the mystic garb over our indigestion.

It would seem that the only real distinction between the night of sense and that of spirit is one of depth. To begin with we possess ourselves little and can give God only what is external, so to speak, our sense area, and God never forces us beyond ourselves. He can get at only what we offer him and this, to begin with, is relatively shallow. This is the night of sense. As we grow under his living touch what we offer is deeper; deeper and deeper reaches come into being and are exposed to him; hence the night of spirit. But growth and purification are not automatic. God's action must be accepted however it comes. I think people are misled by low-key experience: just rather dull greyness, monotony, nothing-to-it sort of feeling. This seems far removed from the torments and desolation John describes so movingly. It is likely to be just as much the real thing; more likely because it is unrecognised.

This last sentence reminds me to say that in these early stages of the spiritual life we cannot know where we are and therefore any pinpointing of suffering — 'this is the passive night of sense' — would in itself indicate the contrary. One might be told by a director that it is so and therefore hold it in a notional sort of way but with no inner conviction. Never would the certainty of it being the result of God's mystic holding spring up from the heart itself. Only later on, perhaps far on the second island, perhaps not until the third, can we know where we are. We can only know where we have been. We need to be very simple. Acknowledging simply that we belong to the common herd, accepting the ups and downs of life, accepting our inner trials from whatever source they come, seeing them all as God's instruments without romanticising.

St John does not want us to cling to suffering. In his teaching on the passive night of sense he makes it clear we must escape from the anguish and move into a night that is tranquil and lovely. This we do by faith. Much of the suffering of this period flows from the sense of going wrong, from growing self-knowledge which is painful, from the overturning of our optimistic and often romantic ideas concerning the spiritual life. Now if we look at God, put our trust in him, accept our misery, sure of his love, much of our suffering goes. We are at peace. This is what we must aim at. Clearly, the key-word is 'trust'. And trust demands humility. Quiet, but unremitting, vigorous trust beyond self cannot be overstressed. This is how we cooperate with God. If we are remiss, if we just slide along, failing to activate our new powers and to live what under his divine touch we have become, then he cannot go on touching us. Many, many people never move from the self, never move into God.

It would be easy I suppose to accept God when he comes as God, but he never does! Too often we take our own idea of God, the fashioning of our pride, as God, but when he comes in the way he always comes, in human helplessness, without beauty and without majesty, we do not receive him. It is easier to accept him in outward events, even humbling ones, but oh, the scandal of the poverty and godlessness of our own inner state. How many accept him in this? Here is true mystical suffering with no vestige of self-esteem. When we stop to think about it, at every moment we are choosing God or self. Put in

another way we are continually being faced with a decision on
God's fate: do I accept him, do I kill him? God always presents
himself to us as man, in the human situation; he does not come
to us divinely, as God — we would not kill the Lord of glory.
But the helpless, ordinary man, this shabby disturber of our
peace and complacency, we must dispose of.

After all, Jesus' contemporaries were not asked to accept
him as God, only to be logical, to recognise and affirm goodness when they met it. They were asked to face and accept
reality, to judge and accept reality as it is, not as one's preju-
dices and fears would like it to be. We see our own reactions in
those of the people who wanted to be left in peace, to get on
with the ordinary business of life without this disturbing man
calling them beyond themselves, saying things they did not
want to hear; of the officials, the denizens of the 'world' out to
defend it against this man who shook it to its foundations; of
the priests with their own image of God, an image fashioned in
their own likeness, a god they could manipulate and cope with.

A man of the people, a helpless man done to death, no one
to speak for him, no one to avenge him — a typical incident in
human history, a history stained with falsehood and cruelty.
But this time it was God. God picked out of human history this
one life and fate to show us the awful significance of our
seemingly insignificant choices. Our evasions of truth, our dis-
honesties — it is God we are killing; our cruelties, unkindnesses
— it is God we are killing. This is the terrible truth, this is fact,
and yet how careless, how indifferent, how frivolous we are. Do
we not need to plead for understanding to see things as they
really are?

It is not difficult to understand how some will be tempted by
the glitter of what certain so-called spiritual movements offer.
These can come much nearer to their preconceived ideas of
what a spiritual life will be like. Their present state is the exact

opposite. To choose what seems a more interesting, even exciting and certainly more satisfying way of drawing near to God is, in fact, to escape from the loving grasp of God and to forfeit total union with him. This temptation is not likely to entrap a person further on, on the second island itself, for here the light from God is too clear.

There will be a great danger of more or less abandoning prayer, even though a certain amount of time is given to it, in favour of activity. 'I'm not a contemplative, I'm a Martha-soul. I can't pray'. Such a one becomes a seemingly generous doer of the word, full of good works, serving others without stint. A most generous person everyone would say. But God sees her as escaping from her poverty and that emptiness of achievement which she experiences in prayer. Now she feels she is doing something really worthwhile, something concrete. She comes to the end of each day tired-out but satisfied she has given herself fully. This temptation is most subtle in a contemplative community where a measure of time for prayer is carefully kept so there is no sense of having given up prayer. But she is far from that total orientation to prayer which is what the contemplative life is about.

This temptation is more insidious because, at this stage of the journey, the contemplative touch is confined to prayertime only, otherwise we could not take it. How often people will tell you that it is outside the time of prayer they feel able to pray and have a sense of God's presence, and that they are with him continually during their work. This feels like the real thing whereas that awful unsatisfactory hour in choir, what good is that to God or man? — that empty futile struggle with distractions? That surely is a waste of time for *me*? It would be a different matter if I could make good use of prayertime, granted then it would be better than activity, but as things are . . .? What is not being realised is that it is precisely at prayertime that God is touching me. What I feel afterwards is relatively unimportant, but whatever is important in it flows from this time of humble, empty waiting on God.

In summing up this state of soul I call the bridge I would remark that it is not a state as the islands are states, but rather a transition. It would be accurate to say, I think, that most of those who walk on the bridge live on the first island. One cannot stand still on the bridge; one must go forward or slither back.

A few really do belong to the second island but have fled from it. More of these later. This transition period is essentially one of activity, that is we ourselves must walk. We are urged and pushed from within but we choose or refuse to walk. All along the bridge God's action is intermittent and light. It does not preponderate. By far the greater initiative rests with us, aided, of course, by God's ordinary help.

We must learn to trust, refusing to set any value on what is felt, whether it be consolation or suffering. If only we learn to cast ourselves into God's care all sorts of things can be amiss with us and they do not matter. I am thinking of St Teresa at this point. She had not a few illusions, as any impartial observer will admit, but ultimately they did her no harm because she handed herself over to God. The same is true of St Thérèse. There were many things in herself she did not understand. Although she appreciated human littleness, her own littleness, it seems she never consciously grasped the deformity and the wretchedness of this littleness. And yet one wonders . . . that profound attraction to the despised and bruised face of Christ, that breakdown in her childhood — did these flow from her sub-conscious knowledge of it? Take that psychosomatic illness of her childhood which we must see as a highly neurotic plea for attention and reassurance. For her sisters and others it was a demonic attack on a child of predilection;

Thérèse accepted this interpretation and so never tasted the bitterness of shame which would have been hers had she seen it for what it was. In many ways Thérèse suffered in the dark. Again so great was her need of Pauline and Céline that she had to overvalue them and not see their weaknesses. In this sense she saw little of the human truth about herself and her context, but this makes the lesson she teaches all the more striking. She had an unshakable grasp of the essence of the matter and this is what we must look at, this is the all-important thing. She just knew, without understanding why, that she must make an irrevocable choice of 'unimportance' whatever happened — unimportance in every sphere, spiritual as much or even more than human. She gave herself wholly into God's hands, trusting in his goodness, not in herself. Had she seen more of the truth about herself it would not have shattered her, for she gave herself to God and that included what she saw and what she did not see, the whole of her, and it was in God she trusted, his love for her, not in her goodness. She reveals clearly that it does not really matter what we understand about ourselves or our context so long as we put ourselves in God's hands. Our problems and difficulties will dissolve of themselves. God coming to us where we are; we surrendering in total trust from where we are, as we are . . . it is simple enough.

4

A LOOK AT 'EXPERIENCES'

What about that massive weight of testimony from men and women down the centuries: that God can be experienced in some way, 'tasted', 'seen', 'felt'? The question must be faced head-on. This will not be an exhaustive treatment of the various phenomena which have accompanied the interior life, which I am not capable of giving. But I want to suggest some basic principles.

First I want to make a distinction between two ways of experiencing mystical union. By this I do not merely refer to full and transforming union, the culmination of the spiritual life, but to those partial unions which happen all along the way, when God touches our being with his own and for that instant unites it to himself. This includes those first early touches when being itself is so dwarf-like that the union is minimal. 'Mystical state' and 'mystic' I reserve for the final union. But in all mystical union from first to last there are two different ways of experience, that I call 'light off' and 'light on'.

To say that, when God touches being with his own being, when he would give himself to us as God, he must necessarily by-pass the ordinary routes into the self and create one for himself which only he can use, is at the same time saying that this visitation, this contact is, of itself, inaccessible to ordinary perception. By the very nature of things it must be secret, hidden. This normal, proper obscurity I call 'light off'. Something unspeakably wonderful is happening in the depths of self and the self cannot see it. No light shines on it. There are effects flowing from this happening and these are consciously experienced, but not the happening itself. 'Light off' is the normal mode.

However, it is possible for God to switch on a light, so to speak, then what is happening is 'seen'. What this faculty is by which we 'see', I do not know. What I want to stress is that the fundamental happening is the same; the switching on of the light does not add to it or change it in any way. For this to be the usual mode of receiving the mystical embrace is exceedingly rare, and this is another point I wish to stress, for I fear it has not been appreciated. A 'light on' state as distinct from an occasional reception of 'light on' may perhaps occur no more than once or twice in an era. It has a prophetic character. The one so endowed understands beyond the ken of human kind and he or she must enlighten others. This light throws its beams on the ordinary way and enables us to understand it. Could we understand it unless 'light on' had lit it up for us? Teresa and John belong to this category of 'light on'. I say this not because of their intense, sublime, emotional states, for these can equally belong to 'light off' but because of their ability to analyse spiritual states. They see what is happening. Take John's analysis of the common-place dryness of 'beginners'. Other writers were aware of this phenomenon and saw it as a trial and testing of the soul, but he saw further. He saw that it was the effect of the mystic touch. What a boon to us this knowledge has been. You have only to compare the writings of St Teresa and St John with St Thérèse to grasp the difference. Thérèse had a wonderful knowledge of God and his ways but she could not analyse what was happening within her as could Teresa and John. For my part I could not have attempted to write this book were it not for the knowledge gained through Claire's 'light on'.

At the risk of anticipating too much I think it will strengthen my position at this point — aware as I am that it may be challenged — to say something of the 'light off' and 'light on' experience of the final stage because it is then most clearly seen. For one thing, it is only in this final stage that 'light off' can really know where she is and what has happened to her. Yes, she knows with deep certitude that she is intimately united to God, and this reality is shown by the way she lives. We have only to recall how certain Thérèse was of her state in spite of the darkness. There is a constant certitude though nothing is seen and nothing is felt. God alone is, filling the horizon and all else. She does not see God: what she does see is herself. Not God enfolding her, not what he is doing, but rather the effect of this in herself. The essence of this state is that God has taken over, despoiled her of her own powers, replaced the ego, and the effect in the psychic, conscious life is one of despoliation, emptiness.

On the other hand, in the 'light on' state, the same basic reality, the union, is not only known with certainty (as with 'light on') it is also seen. It does not fill the consciousness all the time, otherwise life would cease, but the person sees that she is held in God's embrace; the whole being knows it and responds, surrendering to his love. But as it is a question of God himself, this seeing is non-conceptual; it simply cannot be held by the mind, looked at, still less described. I feel this 'light on' state is not understood. How can it be when it is so rare? Unless one knows it by experience it will be easy to confuse it with various psychic states. Here I can only stress again that of its nature it is non-conceptual, and cannot be looked at by the mind.

It is possible for God to switch on the light occasionally for one normally in the 'light off' state. His purpose may be to encourage, to enlighten. . . .It may well result in deeper darkness. Natural light is killed and the springs of earth's joys dried up. Petra has twice known a 'light on' experience, at least, what she considers to be such. More than thirty years lay between. She holds that anyone who has known a true 'light on', however fleeting, will clearly distinguish it from its psychic echoes — the lightning and the echoing thunder. She described the experience as though an abyss opened up within her, an abyss otherwise wholly inaccessible and unknown. But both Claire and Petra are emphatic that this 'accessory' of 'light on' adds nothing to the basic grace. It is the happening that matters, not the mode of experience. What is more, of itself it is no criterion of progress. It is not a reward, not a question of a certain point of progress being reached before God can give it. It can happen at a very early stage if God wills. The testimony of Claire and Petra is significant here. Claire tells me that by the age of five God had become consciously the burning reality of her life. She 'saw' him, the light was on and has remained so. So, in a real sense, her experience of prayer many years ago, at the beginning of her life, is more or less what she experiences now — a non-conceptual 'seeing' God holding her being. She has never known darkness or 'absence'. Here her way does not conform to what authors say! But she points out that it is she who has changed. By nature she would be a selfish person and certainly from what she has told me of her childhood and early youth she was far from selfless. She was not really concerned with people. As God worked in her and she surrendered more and more, she grew in concern for others. I know her most intimately and can vouch for the fact that now there seems no self left in her. She is wholly given.

Petra has always been hidden in the shadows which yet were light. Her emotional experience of prayer now is no different from when she was a child or a young woman. She realises clearly that, as with Claire, the mystic element was present at an early age but she has known nothing but 'darkness', 'absence'. She too does not conform to 'what the books say'! But she too has changed profoundly. Were she to go by what she feels on the emotional, psychic, conscious level, then she would have to say that she is no further on than when she was twenty, or eight years old for that matter.

What I want to demonstrate is the relative unimportance of what is felt. Both Claire and Petra are certain that they are in a state of transforming union. The one 'sees', 'feels', 'tastes', the other simply 'knows'. Though on the conscious level their experience has hardly anything in common there is perfect understanding between them. They speak the same language and enter into each other's deepest self because basically they are in the same state where Jesus is all.

It must be stressed that for neither 'light on' or 'light off' have we claimed any distinguishing 'favours'. This is crucial. What a world of misunderstanding here! It would be a complete misconception to think of 'light on' as a state abounding in 'favours' such as St Teresa describes: her prayer of quiet, union, rapture, ecstasy. The essential experience of 'light on' is non-conceptual, it cannot be handled by the mind. It is indistinct and all-pervading. It has nothing to do with 'things happening'.

But say a 'light on' person wanted to describe as best he could what he saw of God holding the soul, even the first light holding we described, which the soul ordinarily experiences as aridity, then, profoundly moved by what he saw, he might pour out the most extravagant images, all the while knowing that his words were totally inadequate to give any idea of this ineffable, non-conceptual reality. Is there not something of this in the bible imagery? Here the wonder and magnitude of God's direct intervention perceived by the believing heart under its material form is painted in fantastic imagery: mountains skipping like rams, the sea fleeing, heaven and earth rocking and so forth. Possibly this fact accounts for much of the exuberant descriptions of our mystics. However, this is clearly not the whole answer and we must say something more about 'favours'.

Those in both categories ('light on', 'light off') are liable to psychic experiences. We could call them psychic echoes. Basically they are self-induced, not in the sense of self-deception though this is possible, but as rising out of the psyche under certain stimuli. They are not supernatural, not God nor from God. Anything that can be conceptualised or looked at is not God, not the mystical union. This union cannot be appreciated by that range of activities which can look at, take hold of, 'favours'. Clearly God cannot touch someone without changing them, without effects. The essential effects are what count but at the moment we are not concerned with these, only with the secondary, quite unimportant ones. These are of the kind that result from other stimuli: extreme fasting, drugs, aesthetic pleasure and so on. Natural mysticism, as it is called, claims similar phenomena. Human nature, at least in some people, reacts like this. Nothing more nor less than that is involved. Yet it is these utterly irrelevant effects which are considered important and sought after as being identified with the mystical state. They become the criteria by which the reality and depth of the mystical union are estimated. Inestimable loss has been caused by this misconception.

We could think of the recipients' psychological make-up (and here environmental stimuli will play a vital part) as a channel: a deep straight canal, a rocky ravine, a shallow bed — whatever. The over-flow from this grace of union will flow into the channel that is there and take its character from it: phlegmatic, choleric, depressive — reactions will differ widely. What is being revealed is not the grace as such but the psychic 'apparatus' of the person and its reaction to stimuli. When these side-effects are taken for the reality or confused with it, you get a high appreciation of them and hence a desire for them. They are signs of progress, therefore I want them — it can lead to autosuggestion. When the appreciation and expectancy are almost universal then the pressure is enormous and the self-inducement all but inevitable. Where this climate of expectancy is absent in a more sceptical and psychologically knowledgable culture, they are far less likely to happen. You see this in communities, especially enclosed communities. If an influential person within it — a prioress or some other with a personal ascendancy — goes in for 'experiences in prayer', esteems them and communicates her esteem, invariably you will get an outbreak of them. Quite innocently others will produce them. They will become the 'thing', the sign of an authentic mystical life. The tendency will be for those not susceptible to be considered less spiritual, non-contemplative. Reading the early annals of our order I have often been struck by this fact and it surprises me that people do not see the mechanism at work. John of the Cross grasped the psychic character of these 'favours' and hence his uncompromising teaching on detachment from them, yet his own channel allowed an exuberant overflow, a fountain rapturously leaping upwards, a cataract hurling into the dark abyss: but no matter how sublime, not the grace itself.

Since these 'favours' come from the self and are not the touch of God, merely side-effects in certain people, you can get them at any stage, varying in proportion to the stature of the person. It is not impossible for someone on the bridge still running over the first island to experience something akin to ecstasy. God could put the light on, so to speak, and the person would see, in his own small measure, how God loves him, and in his own small measure respond. However, this is unlikely because God sees that, at this stage, he could not use the grace given, could not benefit by it. But he can know excessive delight. It should be clear that the greatest caution must be used in assessing the quality of prayer. Never should what we feel be used as a criterion, and here I mean feelings such as absorption, ecstasy, feelings of union, awareness of God and so on. It is on this point we disagree with St Teresa. If we look at what she says of mansions IV, V, VI, we shall find descriptions of three forms of 'absorbed' prayer. In IV, it is the will alone that is 'held', and this she calls prayer of quiet. In V not only the will, the mind too is momentarily 'held' — prayer of union. In VI the whole person seems carried away — prayer of rapture. Teresa sees here a gradation: the more intense the emotional experience the deeper the prayer. It is this assessment of prayer by emotional intensity that we reject. There is a very true sense in which progress consists in becoming more and more absorbed in God: 'Thou shalt love the Lord thy God with thy whole soul, with thy whole mind and with all thy strength'. A person can be absorbed in this way and yet never know the emotional states Teresa speaks of. On the other hand a person may abound in them and be very far from this total obsession with God.

One of the main reasons why so few attain union with God is because people want these things and seek them and take a secret pride in them. God's touch always produces humility, always, automatically. But all too often these overflows are a source of secret complacency and self-esteem. In reality, they have no positive value. It is the state, not the awareness of the state that matters, and this is not so easy to assess as people think.

It may be well to say more of so-called 'natural mystical experiences' as, in a christian context, they are often taken for the real thing. They have in reality nothing in common with it. They are basically of the same nature as the ecstasy of Words-worth and of other poets. But when they occur in a religious setting, to one who has some faith and is trying to turn to God, they can seem supernatural. A good example of this sort of thing comes in Julian Green's autobiography *To leave before dawn.* Julian is describing an experience of his boyhood: 'A feeling of indescribable happiness swept over my whole being. It seemed as though the threats that weighed on the world no longer existed, that all sadness had suddenly ended, and that, in a deep and complete security everything blossomed into joy . . . I did not think of God. I thought of nothing, to speak truthfully; I did not think. I forgot who I was'. But he goes on to raise the question as to whether this was a touch of God. Over and over again we must stress that mystical graces can be tested only by results, never by what the recipient feels, and on this criterion it is quite clear that this was no mystic grace. When God directly touches being, not only is it drawn to love him but it can also see where and how he is to be loved. The self-deception and blindness of Julian as this stage of his life argues definitely against the mystical. This is not to deny that God does draw souls to himself by this psychic awareness, but without transgressing the limits of the natural. These psychic experiences should not be despised, but on the other hand they must be seen for what they are and not confused with mystical graces. We must always stand in truth and not mistake shadow for substance. Those responsible for the guidance of others should be wary when appraising these accounts. How often we hear 'she can spend hours before the blessed sacrament; God gives her great graces' and the like, whereas sheer facts demonstrate the purely natural sources of these states of consolation. The less attention we pay to what is felt the less likely is delusion and its baleful consequences. 'Unless you see signs and wonders . . .' sighed Jesus. Man has always craved for the grandiose manifestations of God, and in the old testament we see the people mistake the inspired verbal expression of God's intervention for the intervention itself. And in the new, the great, unutterable reality is God coming to us in Jesus, coming to heal our blindness, to give us strength, to cleanse the leprosy of sin, to raise us from the dead. But he comes as a tiny child to share his life with us; a poor, helpless man dying on the cross. How few really accept this. We still crave for the miraculous and 'sublime'.

So far we have referred to consoling overflows or consolations but everything said of them applies equally to suffering ones. Any suffering that we can hold in our hands, give a name to, look at and dramatise is not mystical suffering. It comes from the self and can become 'spiritual riches' just as much as 'consolations'. Indeed I think deception is even easier and more harmful in its consequences, for after all there is a sort of innocence in wanting delight and taking satisfaction in delight. A beginner can know abysmal horror and it has nothing to do with God, though the sufferer will not believe that. Mystical suffering is nameless and the one in its throes would never dream of its origin. It would seem too miserable, wholly 'ungodly' to ascribe a name to. Once again, what God does in us always produces humility; all that comes from self, be it delight or suffering, tends to boost the ego. The touchstone of God at work is profound dissatisfaction with self, a sense of unimportance, whereas 'favours' tend to nourish self-esteem.

It could be objected that on the one hand I keep reiterating that what we feel is of no importance, and on the other hand claim that one particular state of feeling is important. For we are always in a state of feeling. To feel nothing, to feel dry, to feel God is absent, to feel unimportant is a state of feeling, so what? The point really is that the error lies in presuming, in a subjective manner, that what one feels, be it delight, be it suffering, be it dryness, whatever, is a sign of God at work in me. It may well be a side-effect but we can never presume so. One could almost say that the sure sign of God at work — given of course some other obvious ones such as progress in virtue — is that nothing in one's feeling life seems to point to this. A counsellor may tell us so, and thus we may hold it in a notional way, but it won't be a subjective awareness.

When all is said and done, the long line of saints and spiritual writers who insist on 'experience', who speak of sanctity in terms of ever-deepening 'experience', who maintain that to have none of it is to be spiritually dead, are absolutely right provided we understand 'experience' in the proper sense, not as a transient emotional impact but as living wisdom, living involvement. All the truths of faith there in our minds will be translated into practical terms, all we believe becoming principles of action. Thus spiritual 'experience' is as necessary a mark of a loving soul, of a holy person, as medical 'experience' is of a doctor. So often, however, what the less instructed seek is mere emotion. They are not concerned with the slow demanding generosity of genuine experience.

5

THE HOLD-UP

This chapter is given up to examining why, of all those who devote themselves to an interior life, relatively few attain, not only the unitive state but even the illuminative. St John of the Cross declares that, though passing mystical graces are the lot of the many, a state of contemplation is given to few (*Dark Night* 1, VIII and IX). We have no reason for thinking otherwise. As he says, and who would not, this is a lamentable thing and what can we do about it? He ascribes one of the causes to ignorance. Hence this book.

I am sure many will find this chapter discouraging; frankly, it is meant to be. It is meant to discourage us utterly from our own supposed achievements, our own activity and good works, from 'what I am', 'what I do'. But this is only the other side of the coin of perfect trust in God, for whom all things are possible. Thus one cannot enjoy true encouragement and consolation until one has been totally discouraged.

To get the matter clear I would like to recapitulate. We know that God made us solely that he might give himself to us, give himself totally. He does not choose to give himself partially to one, a little more to another, wholly to yet another. He is the giving God; it is his nature to give and he has chosen to give himself to men without reserve. All the obstacles are on the side of man. The sun is beating on the shutters of a window, open the shutters and the room is filled with sunlight. In our response we have to distinguish between 'cannot' and 'will not'. Just because we are finite, just because we come into being only gradually and only in the measure that we respond to God, to begin with we cannot receive God as God, and God gives himself in an indirect way through images, concepts, intuitions, feelings. This is the state of the first island. Through instruction, reading, meditating on the data of revelation and through struggling to do God's will in so far as we understand it, we can grow in trust. We begin to realise a little how worthy of trust God is and the time comes when God can expect an act of dark trust, that is, he can expect us to receive him on his own terms when, in fact, he does come as God. Then he gives himself for a fleeting moment at a deeper level, and now it is himself unmediated he gives; a direct contact independent of the ordinary processes of knowing and loving, and the result, as we have seen, is confusion. Had he come thus earlier, as of course he is always wanting to come, we could not have responded. God in his delicate love never takes us beyond our capacity. He helps us to grow, watches with marvellous concern over our growth, waits patiently for the moment when he can come to us in this special way.

We have only to look at the slow education of the chosen people to see his work. He came to them as they were, condescended to their primitive ideas of him and their crude morality. He did not force himself upon them, did not force growth. When this people had reached a certain degree of spiritual maturity, he came to them in his Son. Who received the Messiah? Only those who were humble and open, prepared to accept God as he chose to come, prepared to believe that he could come in strange ways; those who let him be God and did not insist on being God themselves, on knowing how God ought to behave. These, but also others whose need was great,

the sinners, the wretched — they too were open. We know that
even for the most enlightened there was shock and bewilderment — our Lady, the apostles. The word which sums up his
acceptance is 'faith' or 'trust'.

Who were closed to him? The professionals, the 'good', the
organised religious people. Terrible thought! Why were they
closed? All sorts of subtle ramifications lie behind their
attitude but perhaps we can sum them up in the word
'self-satisfaction' or 'self-complacency'.

If we consider deeply what faith in God or faith in Jesus
means we sense, though perhaps dimly, that it involves a total
dying to self. St Paul points this out. By faith we 'die'. It means
renouncing myself as my own base, my own centre, my own
end. It means so casting myself on another, so making that
other my raison d'être that it is, in truth, a death to the ego.
The whole of the spiritual journey can be seen in terms of
trust, growing in trust until one has lost oneself in God. But we
are mistaken if we think we can do this for ourselves. Not only
can we not do it, we cannot even dream of what is meant by it,
what it is like. True, we grasp the words: trust, giving, no confidence in self, poverty, humility . . . but they are words to us,
though we think we really do grasp the concepts. What we are
talking about is so much part of our fabric that we cannot
stand out of it and look on. It is our way of being to be our own
centre, and we do not realise it until God begins to shift us. It is
only one in whom God has worked profoundly who can see the
difference. The rest have no yardstick.

Our natural, unquestioned reaction to anything which
would reduce our self-assurance is avoidance and a rebuilding
of what has been knocked down. Let spiritual people take
note. Just because they have learned to 'practise humility', to
take slights, disappointments and the rest 'humbly', in other
words have a humble code of action, they think that this does

not refer to them. What I have especially in mind is that true, sickening reduction of self, our sheer unimportance (the 'humility' just mentioned can be a boosting of the ego). It is this we avoid and resist like death. And yet this is it. God is always trying to disturb us. Or rather, he is always giving himself to us, and inevitably the result of his nearness is this disgust with self, but we so hate this that we reject the gift. We do not know that we do, of course. We think we are seeking God when we go after this and after that, all the time building up our spiritual image while he is left waiting at the door.

For God to give himself wholly, according to the full potential of the person, means total death of the ego. At the stage we are still speaking of, the bridge, God is trying to get us to accept a state where we have no assurance within ourself that all is well with us; a state where no clear path lies before us, where there is no way; a state of spiritual inadequacy experienced in its raw, humiliating bitterness. As I write this I know heads will nod assent. How convince people that they have not begun to know as yet? No greater service could be done them than to give them at least a glimmer that they are not spiritually advanced, not, as they too readily assume, on the second island (few would assume that they were on the third). Only too readily, just because they have known some passivity, some contemplative grace accompanied by psychic effects, they think they are in a contemplative state. Over and over again I have seen this happen, and nothing blocks God's grace so effectively. To take for granted we are further advanced than we are ends our progress.

This self-satisfaction — the bane of the professionally spiritual — can be looked at in terms of thraldom to the law. 'The pride of man shall be humbled; God alone shall be exalted on that day'. This magnificent theme of Isaiah, overwhelmed with the holiness of God, is taken over by Paul in Romans as he

struggles to reveal the heart of christianity, the utterly gratui-
tous love of God which comes to us in Christ; that it is God and
he alone who sanctifies us. He was up against it, as our Lord
was up against it in the pharisees, and he is desperate to break
down the resistance. He paints in lurid colours the sinful condition of man and what he is when left to himself, going from
bad to worse. But he has no intention of excluding the jew
from this ugly picture, in spite of his devotion to and pride in
his observance of the law. The jew too has only one saviour.
What is more, the pagan is more open to salvation just because
he is aware of his corruption, as were the publicans and sinners
who came to Jesus; it is the 'righteous', the good people, unaware of the depths of their misery, sheltering as they are
behind their faithful observance of the law, who don't need
God and his saving Christ. They crucify Jesus.

We must be slow to think this no longer applies to us, we
who acknowledge Jesus. Paul's intense words, his scorn, his
pleading, are addressed as much to us as to the jews of his day.
The law which was meant to bring men to Christ has become a
snare. A truly faithful observance of the law, reaching out to
the demands of the sermon on the mount, would lead to a
crippling sense of one's inadequacy before it. By that very fact
we become aware of our need for Jesus, that, as St Paul says, he
has become our holiness because we have none of ourselves.
But what happens is what happened in the case of the jews.
Unable to reach out to the perfect fulfilment of the law, with
its demands of total truthfulness, total self-giving love, we
somehow manage to shut off this vision and create for ourselves
ways, means, prescriptions, ideas, thought-patterns, a whole
mechanism which put into operation makes us, we feel, dead
safe with God. We are so busy with these that we fail to listen
to what God is asking us, now at this moment. I am running
happily on the well-worn track, worn by thousands before me,

good people serving God; I do not need to look further or even to question the direction of the path. We talk about freedom but we don't really want it, as Paul knew. Freedom costs too much, it is frightening, it carries no guarantees; that freedom which makes me utterly and solely responsible to God for my decisions and choices; that freedom which sets me exposed, defenceless before the burning love of God.

We are afraid to trust ourselves to love. We do not really believe in God's groundless, unmerited, eternal love for us. This must be the rock, the solid rock beneath us. God loves me, not because I am good but because he is good. This conviction must be lived out at every moment of the day. God made me in order to give himself to me and he wants nothing of me, literally nothing other than to let him love me, let him pour himself out upon me in everlasting joy. But somehow we have got it into our head, and even when it has gone from our head it is still written into our flesh, that we have to make God love us. We have to make ourselves beautiful in order to be acceptable to him. Did not the old teaching on grace imply this? What I do becomes all important. God is looking on approvingly or disapprovingly at my performance, ready to reward me or show his displeasure. And even those who have outgrown this cruder pattern still place the onus on what we do. If we were to get to the bottom of our attitude, to the motor behind our activity, we would find, shocking though it sounds, an atheism. We have made a god, we have our god but it is not God, not the Father of our Lord Jesus Christ, the loving Father ever pressing in upon us to glorify us with himself; that Father without whom we have no meaning, no existence; the terrible, the holy yet the infinitely tender, who shows us in Jesus what he is. We shrink from the demands of love. Love will stop at nothing, love is not limited by prescriptions, love breaks all bounds, is uncontrollable and unpredictable. We don't like that. We like to be circumscribed, with solid walls around us. We like to know just what we must do and where we must go to be safe from this dangerous God. He mustn't be allowed to get at us, to catch us out in anything. We like to kid ourselves that he doesn't exist. 'Here is your God, O Israel. A God you can cope with, before whom you can feel good, respectable, dignified, successful.'

Jesus came as the disturber of the peace. He challenged the status quo. 'Depart from me I am a sinful man, O Lord', was the reaction of one close to him. He showed up the self-centredness, the godlessness of what passed as religious devotion. He was speaking to the good, and for them his heart was rent. He could not get through. They would not accept him; he disturbed their complacency and sense of security and they had to get rid of him. Oh, we cannot, must not turn away and say 'that's not me, far from it'. Remember we are dealing with something fundamentally human, part and parcel of our humanity, which only grace can deal with and transform. We must let grace in and this we won't do unless we see somehow or other what perhaps we never even glimpsed before; that we are blind, that there are dimensions of existence, of closeness to God, of holiness of which we cannot even dream at the moment, but which are open to us would we but drop our defences, our self-righteousness, our unconscious sham, our desperate need of feeling spiritually successful, and expose our wretchedness and helplessness to God, acknowledging that we do not know him, that we are a failure, that spiritually we have got nowhere.

At that very moment, if we have truly reduced ourselves by standing in the searing light of truth, and if we look only to him, Jesus, our holiness, then he gives himself to us. Nothing then prevents his entering in joyfully as a bridegroom. St John of the Cross points this out over and over again: God is there

like the sun beating in through a window, but so long as the window is dirty and stained, his light can't penetrate; let the dirt and stains be removed and in he streams. This falsity, this complacency and self-satisfaction, this lack of trust are the dirt and stains of the creature that he talks about. Remove them and God flows in and everything is different. (*Ascent* 2, v)
We must pass beyond all created reality, beyond all that we can naturally understand or hope for. We must be detached not only from the goods of earth but from the goods of heaven, spiritual riches. Note what they are: knowledge, taste, security, glory, consolation. Translate them into our terms: the longing to feel safe, to feel good, to feel we know where we are going, that we are successful in the spiritual world, that we are contemplatives, men and women of prayer, abounding in good works.

In case what has been said remains abstract let me try to give some applications. I must confine myself to the situation I know. Do we not confuse the means with the end, seeing observances as though they had an absolute value in themselves? True freedom fixes its eyes on the end and examines the means in its light. There is an openness as regards means; they have only a relative importance. But do we not find ourselves near to panic if some sacrosanct observance is seriously questioned? And are we not, in practice, afraid to say 'yes' to the whole of human reality? Is not fear the motive behind many of our prescriptions? We dare not grow into full womanhood, and if we are superiors we dare not allow our community to grow. There is no knowing what it might lead to. We are afraid of anything involving risk, of anything which might seem a threat to our ideas of what Carmel should be, to the structure which gives us a sense of being right, and on the highway to holiness. But when we think how blind we have been!

In this context I think we have to beware of penance, as a way of escaping from God. This is not so fashionable now as formerly but there does seem a reaction to the present easy-goingness we see around us. Spiritual people are worried at the scorn for penance and austerity and could easily fall into the trap of leaning too much on it. The attitude could grow: 'if I live a very mortified life then I can't be wrong. I have set myself a proven framework of holy living, I have all the traditional know-how and so can't be wrong.' The awful danger is that sticking to this safe framework I feel free from the obligation to listen to God. All sorts of little choices falling to me daily are ignored. I am preferring to follow uncritically the pattern of the good religious. The importance of listening to God hour by hour cannot be stressed too much. Here lies my fidelity, my generosity, here the draining effort to be always there for God when he is giving himself to me. Often enough I am elsewhere, busy about something that means nothing to him.

Nowhere shall we find a clearer instance of a breakthrough out of servitude to the law into the freedom of a child of God than in St Thérèse. The family into which she was born was deeply imbued with a spirituality of work and wages, good works and merits. A careful, impartial study of what we know of this family would destroy any illusion of real sanctity. A standard of behaviour befitting the devout christian was scrupulously adhered to; piety had its rules, its ways of thinking and acting, its proper sentiments and expressions. There was 'heroism', for 'heroism' fits the image of the holy person. Thérèse was reared in this atmosphere. She too learned what she must do, think, feel. Certain reactions were expected of her, and docile child that she was, desperately in need of loving acceptance, she unconsciously produced them. We have only to think of the family's inability to understand Léonie, the member who did not conform to the pattern and produce the right sentiments, to grasp something of the indeliberate, innocent pressure prevailing in the household. We should not take the piety of the young Thérèse too seriously. In great part it was the natural reaction of a child to its milieu, a *sine qua non* of its acceptance. Fortunately it was a devout milieu. There would seem to be no evidence of any mystical state before her entry into Carmel. Hers was the spirituality of the third mansion, our first island. She could have stayed there, but grace was offered and she responded.

Thérèse tells us a lot about herself and we have her letters. But perhaps more revealing is the volume of photographs. A prolonged pondering of these can reveal more of Thérèse than she knew about herself. Profoundly significant is the first one taken in the cloister about eight months after her entry. She is standing by the crucifix in the cloister garth. Thérèse Martin, the little queen, child of predilection as she innocently felt herself to be, is bewildered, full of pain. Everything has gone wrong, is upside down. She is failing. True, she had failed at school, but that was due to her refined sensibility and love of God, not to defect; her family made sure that she should not think otherwise. Now in Carmel she was a failure too. She was not admired. She could not do ordinary jobs well. The Mother Prioress appeared to think little of her. She was quite unimportant, this 'precious' child. But more bewildering, infinitely more bewildering, her lovely feelings of love had gone, she found herself in complete aridity. What was she to make of it? Bewilderment, pain . . . yes, but peace also, peace in acceptance. There is a glimmer of her secret smile even here; she is beginning to understand.

Looked at from our limited human point of view it would seem that God had to get her away from her family before he could offer her his special grace. Would she have been capable

of a response in such an atmosphere? On the very doorstep of
Carmel he met her and she was plunged into darkness. From
that moment we have total fidelity of response in trust and
abandonment. She accepted God on his own terms. She did
not dictate to him. She trusted him, no matter how he came to
her. Light filled her soul and she saw the hollowness of her
spiritual riches. She understood poverty. She renounced what
she had hitherto lived by. It is quite clear that the spirituality
of the Carmel was just as law-bound as that of the family, but
less edifying. Thérèse cut right across it; young as she was she
broke through with what, considering the stranglehold, must
be considered a leap of genius. We know that her ideas upset
some of the 'holiest'. We have evidence enough that even her
own sisters did not understand her. They were convinced of
her sanctity, but for the wrong reasons.

The nuns' depositions during the process for the beatifica-
tion are more a revelation of their own notions of virtue and
sanctity than of Thérèse's holiness. There is a compulsive desire
to show her as flawlessly perfect — contrary to her own emphatic
assertions. Attitudes and actions which, though proof of generosity, spring as much from youthful lack of proportion, are
cited as examples of heroic virtue. Thérèse was to transcend
this but she could not, any more than could our Lord, completely stand outside her own cultural milieu, unaffected and uncon-
ditioned by it. But for her everything was an opportunity for,
an expression of, love for God. There was its only meaning.
Never did she take her stand on good works — only on the goodness of Jesus.

Five years after this photograph was taken we have a series of
others, and we find Thérèse serene, integrated, completely
mistress of herself. We see too her spiritual isolation even from
her own sisters. She is snapped with the community, just one of
them, in no way looking the 'holy nun' and yet, in all the

photographs without exception, she is distanced from them. Undoubtedly this was partly natural. She was not naturally sociable and the photographs reveal this with startling clarity, jolting one into a realisation of the pure love which made her so truly a community nun. But one feels there is a spiritual isolation there, an unfathomable loneliness. She is living in a different world.

So was born the doctrine of the 'little way', born in the most unlikely milieu. Thérèse rejected utterly the cash-in-hand mentality, good works and merit, 'heroism'. Human nature seems to have an inborn capacity to rise to heroism on occasions. It need not denote great virtue. It can be a delusion and induce pride. Christian heroism is Jesus' heroism; the heroism of patience, of accepting what it means to be human, weak, destitute, without resources within oneself. He did not conform to the world's standard of the heroic. It isn't 'heroic' to writhe on the ground as he did in Gethsemane and moan because he had to die. There was no limit to what God could do in Thérèse once she held out her empty hands, abandoning forever any thought of earning or achievement. She opened herself to receive the floodtide of God's love, pent up, waiting for the surrender which would loose the floodgates. Ah, let us keep far away from all that dazzles, she tells us; let us love to feel nothing and have no pleasure in ourselves. Jesus will give himself to us.

I feel I must leave no stone unturned to get across the major cause of mediocrity—lack of trust, and the reverse of this, self-trust. From my own experience in my own situation I can speak of two types of the mediocre religious. First there is the one who has not been faithful and knows it. She knows she has not lived up to the demands of her vocation and makes no secret of it. There is a truth and honesty about her—her saving grace. I have known such a one, as the years go by and old age creeps on with its nearness to death, begin in very simple, unassuming ways to amend, holding out her hands for help. Perhaps death comes before much is achieved and she goes out 'shabby'. She knows she is shabby and trusts in God. I have felt happy at such a death! It is in truth.

But second there is the one who, although she continually evaded the demands of her vocation and in her secret depths knows it, hides it from herself — and others too perhaps — with a facade of spirituality. Possibly she has manufactured some 'contemplative grace' which gives her an assurance of spirituality, of being a success as a Carmelite. I see God prodding this one too. Every now and then she is disturbed, fears rise up, doubts . . . too easily they are pushed away and too easily those around her encourage her in her false peace. She is lucky if she has someone around who will contrive to bring her to the truth and keep her to it, yes, even at the cost of an 'unhappy' death — anything to smash her complacency so that she goes to God with some measure of truth, knowing at least a little of her abysmal poverty. I have been shocked to see how little contrition, searing contrition, features in our living and dying. People say we are blessed to die in Carmel. I wonder . . . It can be dangerous. Only a saint can afford to die the death of a saint. The rest of us need to go out as sinners in our own eyes and in the eyes of our entourage, and our peace must come from trust in God's goodness, not in the complacent but unexpressed assumption that I have lived for God, I am a good nun, I have been faithful.

Because we in Carmel live a protected, structured life, we can delude ourselves that we love God far more than we do. We are faithful religious, and we look perhaps critically at other religious who, as the structures have been relinquished, have foundered. What we need ask ourselves honestly is how many of us, were we to be deprived of our supports and exposed to the 'world', would remain faithful without falling into a puritanical, censorious rigidity. I know I could not remain faithful to prayer day in day out. I know how hard it is to maintain it even for a few days outside our own environment. We do not realise how much of what we think is our virtue and fidelity is in fact conformity. I am not denying the value of supports, but always we need to stand in the truth and see ourselves as we really are. Have we, early or late, reached that single-minded passion for God which Carmel is all about and, indeed, all religious life? When I speak of evading the demands of our vocation, its full implications, this is what I mean.

One of the certain signs that a person is not in the illuminative state is that she thinks she is. Let directors take note. Only in the third state is it possible for the soul to know where she is. A true second-islander will never dream she is that; she will take it for granted that she is of the first island and will be waiting for the night of sense to begin. If she is reading this book she will be taking for granted that everything in this chapter refers to her own mediocrity and will feel no offence at all. Petra's testimony is eloquent here. She told me that sixteen years ago when, as she sees now, she must have been about twenty years on the second island, being without anyone to help her in her grievous desolation, she decided to write to a priest she knew of. He had made an extensive and profound study of the works of St Teresa and St John of the Cross and, what is more, she knew he lived what he taught. She wrote a long, careful and extremely frank letter telling him of the twenty years of her spiritual life. She received an equally long and careful reply in which he took each point of her letter and gave his comment. In substance he told her she could be confident she was in the 'state of union', the fifth mansion (inevitably he used the Teresian terminology) and in our scheme this means the second island. So fantastic did this seem to her that she could not accept it. She could not bear to read the letter twice, so ashamed did she feel, thinking that she had fooled him, taken his time unnecessarily. Intellectually she could see how he arrived at his answer and she felt that she had led him to it. It so passed out of her mind that she only recalled the incident a few months ago. This is typical of the state of a second-islander.

There are others wandering up and down on the bridge who are not complacent. Indeed, while one is actually on the bridge one cannot be complacent, but those souls cannot simply accept their forlorn state and push on. They keep running back to the first island, but because they can find no satisfaction there, they return to the bridge. Their lives can be spent in this way. They are unhappy and suffering but we must not equate the misery they endure with the suffering of the second island. Much of their suffering is due to their lack of real fidelity. They want their cake and want to eat it. They will not resolutely turn their backs on the security of the first island and set their faces to go to Jerusalem.

Before ending this sad chapter on mediocrity, and in case the focus on Carmel has obscured the perspective, I must say something on the church as a whole, the church with her self-righteous complacency, her arrogance and worldliness, who should be showing the world the face of Christ and drawing men to him; a light in the dark forest of human evil, the point of his entry into the world of men, the men he longs to give himself to. Christ suffers in his church. In the passion at least he had his own face, but now he must hide beneath the self-satisfied, ungentle mask men hold up to it. All his beauty is effaced; his authority — 'to give eternal life to all mankind' — turned into tyranny, his meekness into sentimentality, the glory of his passion disregarded under the stress of his bodily

sufferings; his mother degraded to an idol, she herself unknown; his friends taken for mediators with him on our behalf
as though he were not always there for us, total gift; the
sacraments, his presence and saving love, looked upon as
magic or automatic slot-machines.

'Sell everything and give to the poor' is his injunction to his
own, but this the church will not do. She will not make him her
security. She must rely on her own human prudence; jealously
asserting her authority, touchy about esteem, playing safe the
whole time. Yet Peter was called to walk upon the waters. This
is what life for the christian must be; doing what we cannot do,
with nothing to hold on to but Jesus. What a travesty that faith
means a life of peace and security! It is meant to open one to
all anguish, to walk on the edge of the world, with no security
but Jesus.

How mistaken to think that, because the church fails to
reveal the face of her Lord, we must leave her, dishonour and
despise her. She is our mother and ever the beloved of Jesus.
He suffers her patiently and so must we. He gives himself
through her, and will always do so, and we receive him only
through her. To leave her would be to fall into the very sin we
see in her, the refusal to trust God, refusal to live without one's
hands on the controls, the whole while demanding to have
things as I want them, as seem right to me.

Jesus gives himself to men-as-they-are. This is why it should
not scandalise us that the church is as she is and always has
been. One can say, in a sense, that it has to be like that. Jesus
put his church into the care of Peter and at once we have him
failing in trust, succumbing to human respect and fear,
betraying the pure message with which he was entrusted.

But we cannot speak in a detached way of the church. We
ourselves are the church and bear responsibility for her. Above
all it is religious who must bear responsibility for her. God has

chosen them precisely for this, and when one takes that seriously how petty, how absurd is our notion of responsibility:
being entrusted with this job or that. We are meant to be the
prophets of God's people, always listening, always watching.
'What is God saying?' Hearing the word of God and doing it,
we would not have time or energy for petty concerns. This
came home to me in a striking way when I was considering
daily communion. We take it for granted nowadays, and yet
for fourteen centuries the faithful were deprived of it. Who
was responsible for this obscuring of truth, one instance among
many? Who can measure the consequences? Then I thought of
St Thérèse and her understanding, in the face of current
opinion and at the price of being thought presumptuous, that
frequent communion was our Lord's wish, and the courageous
love which drove her to live what she believed. Oh, if we religious lived as she did, with one sole aim of 'pleasing Jesus', the
church's lantern would not be dirty. The light would stream
out in all its purity and men would run to it.

6

THE ROOTS AND BRANCHES
OF SIN

It is significant that when St John of the Cross begins to treat of
the mystical action of God he turns our attention to what are
known as the capital sins. He wants to convince us of our
innate sinfulness so that we may approach God with humility
and self-distrust. He tells us that the habits of sin are so deeply
rooted that only God can destroy them. We must let him. The
mystical action of God gradually reveals these tenacious sinful
habits. We must accept the painful knowledge of self and look
to God alone for healing.

Too easily spiritual people think they are beyond the stage of
considering the capital vices, quite overlooking the tenacious,
all-pervading, profound nature of their hold upon us. They
are perversions of God-given tendencies and are the direct and
terrible consequence of original sin. In their gross form they
are less harmful simply because their grossness offends our
human dignity. It is their subtle ramifications which are
deadly. More harmful than any single, even grave, fault are
attitudes we have adopted, stands we take without realising
their sinfulness.

Covetousness
This is the perversion of our need for security and therefore of
our basic right (because of need) to possess. We religious might

think this is off our plate because we have made a vow of poverty. We have foresworn the right to possess so as to depend on God alone. But do we in reality? Even on the material level we can rely over much on economic security and shut out the disturbing awareness of the poor. And if we are in charge of things we can be stingy and possessive. Everything becomes my own equipment, organisation, time, talent, achievement. I make my nest in religious life. But when you take the spiritual level, why, we haven't begun to depend on God alone, content to have no support but him. If this is not clear to us, think how much it matters to have the good opinion of the community and of authority and how we fall into all sorts of dishonesty rather than lose it. These won't be big things which hit us in the eye, good people will avoid obvious faults, but more in the way of attitudes and motives: my actions, decisions, the opinions I express are really motivated by human respect. I want to be acceptable and often, without reflectiion, unaware that I am merely following and falling in with current opinion without a responsible examination of the facts, I live by what others think and say and truly know not what I live by. These others may not be the community but outside 'authority'; the prestige of the safe, unquestioned stand. My faith remains unexamined because, at bottom, I fear the conflicts which too deep a scrutiny would raise, and how quick I am to censor those who have the love, reverence and trust to explore the content of faith. Possibly the temptations in this area are greater in an enclosed community than elsewhere, but these tendencies are universal; it is their manifestations which will differ. If one holds a position of authority by community vote, what a temptation to please in order to continue to enjoy their prestige! When we really get down to it, are not many of our good actions, what others might call our generosity, inspired more by the desire to feel good than by real love of God? The way we worry about spiritual failure, the inability to pray, distractions, ugly thoughts and temptations we can't get rid of . . . it's not because God is defrauded, for he isn't, it's because we are not so beautiful as we would like to be. How difficult it is for us to grasp in a real way, a way we live by, that we must take the risk of relying solely on the goodness of God. Covetous as we are, we want to have our hands full, want to have something of our own, not God's but ours, which we can bestow upon God or at least hold out to him should the worst come to the worst, and thus claim the reward of heaven.

Envy

'It is not good for man to be alone'. We have an absolute need of others if we are to grow to full personhood but we need others in order to squander ourselves upon them. We grow by loving and this means giving. But we want others only in so far as they build us up. There is a poison in our system, and this lovely thing, community, is contaminated. What should give us joy — the beauty, virtue, talents of others — makes us feel deprived. Another's gain is my loss, I am diminished by your greatness. The good of others is not seen as something to delight in, but as a threat to me, and hence the readiness to find fault, to cut down in size anyone who seems a threat to my self-importance. We can find all sorts of honest motives for this miserable behaviour: it can look like zeal for the welfare of the community, and all the while there is a snake at the bottom of my soul. I think superiors especially need to watch out for this, the temptation delicately to expose another's weakness. It is not easy for a superior to want a rival and nothing is nearer to hand than the opportunity for this gentle under-estimation of a possible one. Little people are accepted easily enough, but any excuse is enough to reveal the hidden flaws of those who are in some way a threat or a challenge. How quickly we see

their minor flaws, we want to find fault, to take the lustre off
their virtues by recalling shadows of the past. What injustice
there can be in a refusal to forget the past and to allow for the
transforming action of grace. Just because we live at close
quarters where every defect is revealed we can be cruel to one
another, yet without apparent gross uncharity. When jealousy
appears in its ugly colours then we renounce it, but so often it
is there unrecognised. We are wanting others on a low level so
that our virtues can shine, or at least the smallness of our own
attainments is then not felt so keenly. This can happen when
the younger generation are getting opportunities which were
denied to us. We don't like it, it makes us feel deprived. We
had a hard time and so must they. We are not likely to formu-
late it in this way but it is there under cover of 'keeping to the
sacred tradition', 'need for complete renunciation', and so
forth. There is no love in envy. Rather than not be special to
the beloved, whether this is God, the community or a friend,
we would prefer to have no one mattering to them. Me or
nothing, says envy. Life for the envious becomes a weary
struggle to attain the unobtainable, with all the accompanying
bitterness and self-reproach. All the same, it is shot through
with self-satisfaction, nicely concealed under the cloak of
concern for the community and for the truth. But the truth
about others is known only to God. He asks us to love them,
that is all. Only when our office or some other claim makes it
our duty to form a tentative judgment may we do so, and then
it must always be with love. Only love can find fault.

Gluttony
Not many of us are tempted to stuff ourselves at table but it
would be a mistake to confine gluttony to this abuse. Fundamentally it is the abuse of God's lovely gift of pleasure, his dear
and delicate wish that we should delight not only with our

minds but with our senses. Everything speaks of him but gluttony cannot listen; gluttony devours, everything is fodder and no more; things are never seen as they are. Gluttony lives for 'experience'; as C. S. Lewis says, the fatal word is 'encore'. There is more interest in experiencing than in what is experienced, and this applies to everything, material and spiritual. We nuns can think far too much about our bodily comforts, food, sleep, draught-free rooms, recreations, reading, chitter-chatter — in a word, in seeing, hearing, feeling, tasting. God wants us to have sense-pleasures, it is one of the ways his love comes to us, to us his body-soul creatures. We have to receive them reverently as the revelations they are and then leave them behind. It isn't only that gluttony steals and defiles them, gluttony seeks self not God. It can't say 'no' to pleasure. If prayer is self-satisfying then the more the better; if we get a kick out of penance, well let's have a lot of penance, all of course with a nod at God, but it is myself I am really seeking.

Anger

The heart of anger is a rebellion against what it means to be human, against God and his deepest will for us. Jesus came to shoulder the burden of being human and opened himself fully to its implications. This is the essence of obedience, the whole-hearted acceptance of humanness. There is a sentence in the *Imitation* about the patience of Jesus being the purest expression of his love for his Father and for us. This is the very antithesis of anger. Anger perverts God's gift to us of free will and the dominion of the world. God wants us to rule as he does, in loving accordance with the nature of things. Anger is impatient of the independent realities around us and attacks them when they do not accord with what we want. Things, events, people, we batter at them if they baulk us. Sometimes the irritation bursts into the open and we let fly, but quite

often pride (especially in 'the good') or temperament prefers to
cover it up and seeks another outlet, dignified coldness and
reserve. We indulge in self-pity at the way life is treating us.
Without facing it we harbour a secret resentment against God
for the way he orders things, but it would be shocking for us
spiritual people to admit this even to ourselves, and so we start
blaming ourselves. Surely God would prefer us to be honest
like Job and Jeremiah and tell him what we feel. But the
terrible danger is that we take our revenge on God by refusing
to trust him, and thus live in great unhappiness. How few of us
really believe in God's longing to be our joy, to flood us with
happiness, and his readiness to turn the world upside down to
do good. The only possible happiness lies in letting him love
us, and everything that has happened and will happen is only
for that purpose. We do not believe God's word.

Lust
It would seem that few religious, or spiritual people in general
for that matter, fully grasp what a block to God's transforming
action lies in refusal to face up to and integrate our sexuality.
The mention of the word 'lust' and automatically we switch off
—that does not concern us. Not as the full act certainly, but
there is more to it than that. Lust is the dishonouring of our
sexuality and there are many ways of doing that. Jesus was
moulded the manliest of men and often enough we are afraid
to accept our own pattern, be it man or woman, and live it out
for the glory of God.

God can only get at us in the measure that we are 'there'. If
we hide from him by failing to integrate vast areas of our
being, then we can never be transformed into him. Grace
cannot find scope in a half-person, which is what we must be if
we do not develop on the human level. Sexuality is essential to
being human; to fail to acknowledge this in practice is to live

away from truth. We meet God and God meets us only in what is real.

Being sexual basically means I am a half and not a whole; it means accepting the fact of incompleteness, and this incompleteness involves pain. Not only that, there will always be the tendency to seek my other half. For the love of Christ and because he has asked us for this, we have renounced the use of our sexual powers, the right to marry, to have children, to be made whole by another. This means having to face and cope with the pain of a raw surface for many a long year, until God fills up the spaces on every level and we become whole in him. He promises to do this and we must live in hope of him alone. The danger is that we try to get rid of the pain, stifle the feelings of emptiness, even deny that they are there (for to admit them doesn't fit the image of the holy nun for whom God is enough), and compensate for what we have given up. This frustrated longing comes out in all sorts of ways—domination, maternalism, passive docility, crushes (normal enough in adolescence, but wholly reprehensible in the adult as a dishonest way of coping with sexuality—getting the thrills of flirtation without any commitment in what seems a safe situation), pseudo-mysticism—and what shabby compensations they are!

A woman is meant to be all-receptivity, all-selflessness, wholly intent on giving and loving, that others may become themselves. A servant and a queen, a queen in as much as she is a servant. We can shirk the implications of selfless love, becoming old maids or frustrated wives-and-mothers. The old maids avoid all personal involvement without which they cannot grow. They are afraid to make friends, though this motive is well disguised by talk of detachment and the undivided heart. They play safe. The frustrated wives-and-mothers have never faced the truth about themselves, and so have lived not on God but on compensations, using their friends, seeking gratification in them, but this time under cover of holy freedom and human fulfilment.

We must struggle through fire and blood to love purely. It will involve searing suffering and this we shirk. Conflict, struggle, disturbances, these we need not fear. To be feared is that blindness and complacency which in the name of recollection, keeping one's heart wholly for God alone and so on, refuses to live, to grow up, become a full woman assuming total responsibility for my own life with its choices and decisions, knowing the principles by which I live, allowing no one and no thing to turn me from them. Inimical to true development is subservience to authority. Obedience is one thing, subservience another.

Pride and Sloth

Pride and sloth together form the tap root from which the other sins branch out. They pervade them all. Respectively they pervert two complementary aspects of reality, that we are very small before the great God, his creatures, but on the other hand, we are made in his image and therefore of infinite value. He loves us and this is our value.

If we think sloth is just laziness, we have minimised it out of all recognition. It can be the most energetic who are the most slothful. Sloth is a distortion of the true unimportance that all men must feel before their maker, and its reaction is to elude right responsibility. I feel that the total demands and promises of God are not for me and therefore do not hold myself responsible in failing to meet them. Each of us has a human responsibility sharpened and coloured for each of us by special vocation. Sloth evades this often by the fever of its own activity. Sloth is very readily 'satisfied', readily says to itself that I keep the Rule, am a faithful nun, am helpful to others, undertake work cheerfully, what else is expected? All this gives no right whatever to say enough, 'I am giving you enough, Lord'. Of course we would never articulate this even to ourselves but deeds speak louder than words. The total giving of love is too much for it, it will not, when we really get down to it, take the trouble. There are no holidays, no loopholes in love, no private little areas for myself. Sloth wants all these, though under different names. That is why activity, whether physical or intellectual, can give the slothful such comfort. It blocks out the demands of love, which always looks not to what we do but why.

Pride distorts the nature of our true value. We can follow all the traditional paths of humility and still the citadel of pride remains unshaken. Pride refuses to accept its poverty. The proud cannot bring themselves to hold out empty hands to God, they insist on offering virtues, good works, self denials, anything in order not to have nothing. They want to be beautiful for him from their own resources, whereas we are beautiful only because God looks on us and makes us beautiful. This is repugnant to pride. God cannot give himself to us unless our hands are empty to receive him. The deepest reason why so few of us are saints is because we will not let God love us. To be loved means a naked, defenceless surrender to all God is. It means a glad acceptance of our nothingness, a look fixed only on the God who gives, taking no account of the nothing to whom the gift is made. To lose ourselves like this is the most radical of despoliations because the last shred of self-importance is discarded. The very words and acts of humility can be a barricade of well-nigh infinite subtlety. Jesus came to us precisely to break down the bars, something we could never have done of ourselves. Yet we cannot live the life of Jesus unless we consent to leave our own pitiful lives, and this is what pride finds unendurable. Striving for 'perfection' is the most disastrous of the mistakes good people fall into. It feeds the very vice it intends to destroy. Most fervent souls are prepared to give God any mortal thing, work themselves to death, anything except the one thing he wants, total trust: anything but surrender into his loving hands. 'You must become as little children', whose one virtue is that they know they are unimportant.

Not only is there within us the basic will to autonomy, to be in charge of our own fulfilment, but this pride is reinforced immeasurably by fear and guilt. Fear is native to man, it arises from his dependency and helplessness. Trust, which alone can deliver him from fear, is killed at its roots by guilt. We feel God cannot love us and therefore we are proud, we stand on ourselves and refuse to let go. More often than not this fear goes unrecognised, especially by people who are more naturally secure and self-possessed, as we say. Yet lurking in all of us, secure or insecure, is an appalling insecurity which must be tracked to its lair. Divine love longs to deliver us from the anguish of our situation but we will not let him. We even refuse to acknowledge the desperate nature of our plight. An emotional appreciation of this, natural to some sensitive temperaments, is not in the least necessary. Many have this emotional awareness of our dilemma, as is witnessed in so many ways today, and yet they do not surrender to God but rather become more and more entrenched in their despairing selves. We are speaking of deeper realms than feeling. There will be continual occasions, in quite sober dress as well as more dramatic, which God is using to bring us to an acceptance of our poverty, but we evade them. Is it not true that most men and women spend their lives running away from fear or, to express it less dramatically but none the less really, from feeling unimportant? We are always on the run, away from what is our peace and perfect security: status, success, role-playing, pseudo-mysticism, these are some of our avenues. We only half-live, touching reality here and there, more or less in a world of illusions. Much of what John of the Cross has to say on mystical suffering has to do with this: the uncovering of this basic anguish that we may surrender to God in poverty. Deep, deep is this self-possession. We are our own enemy. Jesus is our blessed answer. He has taken our guilt upon himself and exorcised fear. Only trust in him, cleaving to him, making him our wisdom, and holiness sets us free.

I shall end this chapter with a short parable, illustrating what I have tried to say. A king had three servants. One day he called them and told them that the ancestral law of the kingdom required that each of them must sit an examination, the importance of which could not be emphasised enough. To call it a matter of life-and-death was a faint approximation of its urgency. Further, and here the king warned them not to lose heart until he had finished, he had seen the examination and could tell them it was wholly beyond their powers. Not one of them could even begin to answer it. In fact, there was only one man in the entire kingdom who could do it and that was his own son. But the whole point of the exam was that they were not expected to do it unaided. The king's son was there precisely to come to their help, and with him, they could be completely confident. He would give them all the answers, and all they had to do, on their side, was to be ready at his palace gates for whenever he should have time to speak to them.

Each servant reacted differently. The first felt the king need not be taken literally with his talk of life-and-death. He was willing to give most of his free time to the business but he was a busy man with important things to do, quite apart from deserving necessary relaxations. So he spent a few hours after supper outside the palace gates most nights and heard some of the prince's explanations. But, of course, he missed what was said at other times and so made a poor showing at the examination.

The second servant thought the king had not sufficiently taken into account his intelligence and general knowledge. He was an educated man and need not, surely, rely on another, king's son or no. So he decided to consult the prince on a few tricky points which were beyond him — which he most diligently did. But not even realising what the questions implied, he missed the point in most of them and did badly.

The third servant believed his master in literal truth. He sent a message to his home that from now on he would be camping at the palace gates so as never to miss a chance of being summoned. He was cold out there, wet often, bored and despondent, especially when days went by without the prince sending for him. But he stayed on tenaciously, and the prince was able to tell him all he needed to know. And this servant answered in full every question in the examination.

7

THE SECOND ISLAND

I can think of no better way to introduce this island than by
quoting a letter written to one travelling across it.

Your letter, with its cry of desolation, goes to my heart and I
long to comfort you. I have the means, for I know well that
what is causing you such grief is, in reality, untold blessing
and yet I haven't the means because whatever I say, though
it may comfort you for an hour on the emotional level, can
only be held by you notionally, in a far-off sort of way that
brings no felt consolation. If you could see but for a moment
what is happening, you would simply die of joy and clearly
God doesn't want that, not yet!

You say everything you read increases your sense of being
wrong, being a failure, being simply nowhere in the spiritual life. It discourages you to read St Teresa and St John, so
remote from theirs does your own poor state seem, but it
isn't only the mystics of a bygone age that produce this
feeling but the words of our Lord himself. Oh, M—, how
many words of Jesus I could quote, how much of Paul, to
show that you are in a good way, that you are treading the
way he trod, dying with him and in that measure living his
risen life. But the words you pick on: 'he who loves me will
be loved by my Father, and I will love him and manifest my-

self to him'. But you cry 'I wanted to love him, I have never
over the long years felt I loved him and he is and always has
been total darkness to me. It is mockery to say he has mani-
fested himself to me. To Teresa, yes, to John, to the other
mystics but to me?' But, my dear, it is precisely because he
has shown himself to you, does show himself, reveal himself,
give himself, whatever word you like to use that you feel as
you do and that you suffer so. What is the essence of your
grief when all is said and done? Isn't it two things: a sense
that you lack God, call it absence, call it abandonment, and
at the same time a devastating awareness of your own
wretchedness. Oh, I know, not in the least like what John of
the Cross writes about, that is what you are hastening to tell
me, nothing grandiose like that, just drab, petty meanness
and utter ungodliness. Yes, but that is what he is talking
about. Thus, as I said at the beginning, your grief is flowing
from immense blessing, Jesus manifesting himself to you.
He is showing himself to you at a depth within you that your
consciousness — your senses, your emotions, your mind —
simply cannot register. It is your deepest self that is seeing
him, that 'knows' him in the biblical sense and is ravished
with love for him, so ravished that he has become an obsession. You can't forget him morning, noon or night and yet,
poor little you, none of this is experienced 'up above'. You
feel anything but ravished with love. You feel bone dry,
bored stiff and utterly miserable. Don't you see why? If your
deepest self keeps getting a look at him, more, is being
clasped to his heart from time to time, then all thoughts and
ideas — and these are what your poor nature is wanting to
relish — are just cardboard. Your poor surface nature is
starved, but your surface nature is not *you*.

Don't you see too that, if you are seeing Jesus, if the Holy
One enfolds you then you are bound to feel with appalling

pain that you are sinful. 'Depart from me for I am a sinful man'. You could never see this before. Oh, I know we think we do, we think we know we are sinful and wretched and so on but we don't. It is only when Jesus comes to us in this sort of way that we see it and it is very, very hard to bear until we grasp the full significance of it and then it becomes our joy. It is really this, a fundamental choice: will I let Jesus be my holiness and stand in the blazing truth, or will I insist on having a holiness of my own—to offer him, of course, to be pleasing in his eyes? The whole essence of the christian demand is to let God be our God and refuse to be God to ourselves. And this is what you are being faced with in a very deep way now. You can say 'no' and it won't seem a 'no', it may seem the utmost generosity. You could kill yourself with penances and good works, you could make sure that not one iota of the law is unfulfilled, you could guard against any possible failing and make quite sure you have no need of a saviour, of a Jesus. You could present yourself before him a worthy bride. Isn't that what we are trying to do secretly? And can you see what I am trying to say, the orientation we must make? It consists fundamentally in a total acceptance of the bitter experience of our poverty and an obstinate refusal to evade it; to accept to stand, in very deed not just in pious imagination, stripped before the living God, our leprosy laid bare, crippled in limb, blind, deaf, dumb—a living need. How few will live thus and let him be their saviour, their life, their light, their food and drink. We want to feel holy, to feel we are really spiritual with deep understanding and insight, pure and noble of heart. 'You alone are the holy one' is the cry of truth and happy those for whom it is the truth they live by. This is what is being asked of you now, my dear. Can you accept it?

Here we have expressed in a living context what is happening in us: 'Jesus is manifesting himself to you. He is showing himself to you at a depth within you that your consciousness, your senses, your mind, simply cannot register'. This showing ravishes us with love. It is the mystical encounter or infused contemplation of which we have said so much. However, it is no longer a question of now and then, as on the bridge, but a contemplative state in which these encounters are frequent, regular, normal. Still, they are only visits, not a permanent abiding.

We learn too that what we experience of these visitations is basically the same as on the bridge: aridity, and a painful knowledge of self, only now these are more diffuse and deeper. This is the island of light and pain. Of pain precisely because of light, light that seems 'intolerable darkness'. Now we see ourself as we really are. We see the hollowness of what we conceived of as our goodness, our truth, our virtues, generosity and achievement. Here, on this harsh terrain, we see in terror and dismay that every road to spiritual success and achievement is blocked. Our cherished ambitions are unmasked and we are called to renounce them completely. All illusions are shattered. The light on this island is remorseless and shadowless, blinding, searing, cruel light. Not only do we see ourself but we glimpse too something of what it means to have nothing but God. Speaking of the first island one might call the experience that of 'godhead', the virtuous, good man feeling in control of himself and his life, everything possible to him. On this bleak island 'manhood' is experienced: what it means to be man and there is nothing glorious in this. It is to feel 'no-man', a worm, a poor mis-shapen beast. All that made him man and gave him dignity seems overthrown.

As to what we must do, and the dangers and ways of escape from God's action, what was said of the bridge is applicable here. A little more must be added. We must understand that this island is a completely different world from the first. As I tried to say when presenting the image of the islands, there is no intrinsic connection. Each represents a wholly different relation to God. The second is not just a highly developed form of the first; one cannot, of oneself, grow into the second. One must be taken there and this 'taking' is represented by the bridge. It is absolutely the only way to the second island, dependent on the divine initiative. I accept to walk on this dark and difficult path he puts me on; or, to change the metaphor, I respond to the life-giving touches of God and grow.

This is a rugged land and perilous. It is not only that it feels perilous, it is perilous in that all the way across its surface one can turn back, and the consequences of turning back are immeasureably greater than at an earlier stage. Needless to say, humanly speaking, the temptation to turn back is overwhelming but the soul is not alone. She is being given strength and deep comfort to persevere. It is characteristic of this island that there can be no half measures. So near is God and so terrible that unless we say 'yes' all the time and accept the conditions of life on this island we must return, otherwise life would be intolerable. What precisely are the conditions? Consenting to have no security but God and him unseen, unfelt, resolutely choosing him and abandoning self, always, all the time. Many people have times when they really see that they can do nothing without Jesus, that they are truly helpless and only one way lies open before them, that of casting their whole weight on him; for a time they do this but it does not last; their trust wavers, they lose courage, they want some toe-hold on security, some assurance that they are getting somewhere. 'I want to live a spiritual life, I want God not *that*: *that* has nothing to do with God', and back they go to where there is a sense of human dignity, of 'godhead'.

However, the 'yes' of a person on this island is by no means total; it is in proportion to their capacity and stage of growth. We are still ourself, though continually supported and guided by God. We can express it this way: at prayer we 'hear', mysteriously, inaudibly, the 'yes' of Jesus. It is not yet our 'yes' for we are not transformed into him, but at least we can now 'hear' it, and know, in some bewildered fashion, what 'yes' means. If we are true, our whole day becomes an attempt to re-echo that 'yes'. Having heard it we now know our own attempts to be absolutely futile; our own 'yes' is heard in all its meagreness at last. Yet we long for nothing else but to go on trying. We know instinctively that our feeble attempts are what make it possible for Jesus to say his 'yes' in us. They both develop and prove our willingness to submit to the terrible kenosis that this involves. It means facing up to the whole range of truth: what God is, what we are. . . .

There is indeed a disconcerting, nay agonising, bewilderment on this island. It is due to the fact that God is 'coming' to us in two ways. This duality is obviously not present on the first island, nor is it present on the third, where there is no coming but permanent abiding. But on the second, the mystical coming and knowing which ensues makes all other knowledge seem empty, and yet it is by this we must shape most of our conduct, for this is all we can possess. Somehow it rings false. We feel we are living, secretly, by another knowledge but this we cannot grasp. We are still in ourself, receiving God as from without; still on our own, God's co-worker only. Hence the sense of being torn, divided, false.

This island comprises a huge expanse and our experiences in crossing it will vary greatly. There is a vast difference between one just arriving and one who, practised throughout long years in willed surrender, is about to depart for the third island. No matter how great the generosity of the traveller their stay here will be long. It is a case, literally, of being undone and remade. Man cannot see God and live. On this island we are 'seeing' God and dying a long-drawn-out death. Our work is precisely that of striving throughout the day and every day to give to God what we could not but offer without reserve in the brief moments at prayer when he held us captive. Not only are we resolved to do God's will, we perceive more and more where it is. This is the island of light, and this living wisdom is characteristic of it. If it is absent, we can be sure we are not dealing with one in this state.

Faith is being freed from the limitations to which it was subject on the first island when the mind had to search for and examine revealed truth. Now faith supplies the content. It is God himself, in himself not an image, that is known and loved though in darkness. This knowledge is not 'outside' us but of our substance. The mysteries of Jesus formerly seen from outside and consciously made the principles by which one must guide one's life, are now our own life; we are living the mysteries of Jesus — progressively, of course. We may be quite unable, at least at times, to look in any meaningful way upon these mysteries simply because they have become our life. For instance, we may assist at mass in deep aridity, unable to 'enter into it', but our life is the mass, an ever-growing surrender with Jesus to the Father. Likewise the Trinity is no abstract notion but living truth. We are in the trinitarian stream — to the Father in Jesus through the Spirit. The mystery of suffering, the folly of the cross is ours, and thus with other truths. At times our mind may be able to grope after what we understand in an incomprehensible way, in order to give of our light to others, but as often as not this conceptualisation will leave us completely arid. We may know we are feeding others but feel starved ourself.

I do not think I will be alone in finding that one of the

biggest difficulties in prayer is knowing what to do with the mind, and the following considerations may help others as they have helped me.

In the first place we have to accept that thinking is the function of the mind as hearing is the function of the ear. My mind cannot but think unless I am in a state of stupor or unconsciousness. God can suspend our thought but this rarely happens. The mind must think but the point is that its thinking has different degrees of importance. In the early stages, that of the first island and to a considerable extent on the bridge, thinking is very important, and on the whole there is no problem simply because the mind is occupied in a way proper to it. The trouble really begins with the onset of mystical prayer and increasingly so. In the state we are considering now, thinking will have no importance at prayer time, indeed it would hinder God's work, but we cannot stop the thinking process. The thoughts won't be of God — these hold no attraction — they will be what we call distractions. St Teresa has a great deal to say on this subject and expresses vividly the distress and anxiety the activity of the mind can cause in the contemplative state. (*Mansions* IV, 1)

There will be a great temptation to abandon or curtail prayer, or to give the mind something to occupy it. There would be no harm in giving it something to quieten it — a vocal prayer perhaps — provided we give this no attention. Our energy must be concentrated on surrendering to God, just as we are, bearing the weight of helplessness and poverty. 'Let the mill clack on while we grind our wheat' says St Teresa. It is intention not attention that is all-important. Intention is within our power; attention is not. It takes courage and trust to pursue this path and the assurance of a guide would be a great help. Yet whatever reassurance is given will have a temporary effect only. Whatever is heard or read which should, objectively, convince us we are in the right way — for example: it can be taken for granted that dryness is at least partially the result of God's action in anyone leading a really dedicated life — will have scarcely any effect. 'But I'm not sure I am leading a dedicated life'. A typical reaction of one in this state. In earlier stages we would most likely presume it. So ultimately we are thrown back on God alone. There is nothing in ourselves, in our conscious awareness to support us. We have no alternative, if we would go forward, to trusting God absolutely. 'If I am mistaken, he is faithful and will show me. Anyway, I'm convinced that this act of trust in itself is pleasing to him'. It is indeed, it is what he is working to elicit. It is all that matters to him.

I was talking over this matter of the mind with Petra and she said it was a long time before she grasped in a real way that what we experience of mind and will is more or less physical. Intellect and will, we are told, are the highest faculties of man and here they are reduced to total inertia in what matters most! I can understand her worry, seeming to become not more but less human. Only painfully and gradually did she become aware that the self can be immersed in profound prayer, can be living intensely in God with no repercussions in the conscious mind and no conscious desire for him. Once she had 'seen' this it made all the difference. That we are most truly praying when we do not know we are, makes sense in this context. However this 'glimpse' of the self in its fathomless depth and occupation, though useful, is not essential. The majority may never know it and perhaps it was given to Petra only that she might clarify it for others. Claire sees it all the time and her testimony has helped Petra to understand it better. This awareness is of no conseqence in itself; trust, not perceiving, is the only answer; trust in the God who never disappoints.

Petra also recalled her discouragement when she read such passages as these: 'the soul that would find him must go out from all things in will and affection, and enter into the profoundest recollection, and all things must be to it as if they existed not . . . forget all that is thine, withdraw from all created things and hide thyself in the secret retreat of the spirit'. (*Spiritual Canticle* I) Such a state of recollection was beyond her! Then she realised that John of the Cross was writing of a deeper level than the mind and conscious memory. He was meaning the deep self and its total orientation towards and choice of God alone. This can be there — the deep self in deepest prayer — when the mind is distracted. And is not the voiding of the memory that John makes so much of, especially in relation to the virtue of hope, along the same lines? If one sees memory as the root of self-identity, then the contemplative action of God will strike it fiercely and the self must correspond with this action of God. We must refuse to recall what we have done for God or how well others think of us; of past 'favours' which seem to validate progress. We must refuse to fall back on anything of ourselves to give us some sense of spiritual achievement when God is despoiling us and inviting us to stand in naked truth. Nothing must be left to us save the unfailing goodness of God.

At this stage of progress we must be active and faithful in rejecting these seemingly reassuring memories. Later on, in the third island, self-forgetfulness is complete. In a very real sense we are there lost to ourself. But this is the direct work of God to which we can give nothing but consent.

This second island corresponds with St Teresa's IV, V, and VI mansions (though possibly some of what she says of mansion IV belongs to the bridge); to the first part of St John's *Spiritual Canticle* up to XX ; and to his passive night of spirit. A superficial reading of the *Canticle* can leave one with a haze over the eyes before the sheer joy of the illuminative state, but read again:

> The source of the grievous sufferings of the soul at this time is the consciousness of its own emptiness before God — while it is drawing nearer and nearer to him — and also the thick darkness with the spiritual fire which dry and purify it.
> He is to it intolerable darkness.
> The soul feels itself as it were in the land of enemies.

Many passages lifted out of the *Canticle* could be taken as coming from the dark night of the spirit. They are, in fact, one and the same state with a different emphasis. (cf *Canticle* XII, XIII, XX, XXI and *Dark Night* 2, VII)

Whilst referring my reader back to all that was said in chapter 4 on 'experiences', this is the time to say something more specific on the phenomena abounding in St Teresa's life. She gives us an apron-full in mansion VI. Has anyone else told us so much about herself as Teresa? Not only have we her autobiography and letters, but her treatises are autobiographical. And yet we have made her a legend. We have made her into what we want her to be, as her own contemporaries began to do. With them, if she fell down the stairs, it was the special activity of the devil, if she had a hunch, it was the Holy Spirit. How often we read of her shrewdness in judging character. Yet she was not only not shrewd, she was a hopeless judge. Time and time again in the *Foundations* and *Letters* she reveals her gullibility. How she swallows, to give just one example, that most obviously neurotic Beatrice, and then we see the painful but surprisingly gradual awakening. Or that matchless Prioress of Alba who turns out years later to be a disaster. The list is endless, and what we have no evidence for in the *Letters* we know from history, as with her tragic misreading of Doria.

These facts are mentioned just to highlight how we misread her.

Teresa was an extremely lonely woman. The incapacity to understand others, and her good-humoured contempt of women, reveals this isolation. She was an eagle in a hen-run. Unconsciously her need for the stimulus of free and educated thought led her to dependence on her confessors. She explains it as but a spiritual need, but it was a craving for the sinewy strength of the male. Poor, lonely Teresa, who had no one to explain her to herself, and who shrank from the one man who could have broken the trap of her temperament. How wildly she was torn by her desires and instinctive drives is indicated by her many psychosomatic ailments and illnesses. She does not seem to have been of a contemplative temperament, one who could be walled up in her cell and find in God all she needed. She was not naturally passive. Her psychic pressures forced her, wholly unconsciously, to manufacture 'experience'. Why should we not see her locutions and visions as this? It does not diminish Teresa, it makes her all the greater as a torn and suffering woman. Some of her favours are false on their own evidence; locutions that refer to events that never, in fact, happened. All those relating to Gratian, so obviously from her own subconscious, make a mockery of God's intervention. And surely we must see her relationship with Gratian for what it was, a crying maternal longing to have this lovely youth for her very own. A revelation of frailty. If some of these visions and locutions and miraculous interventions are proved to be delusions, why not all? It may be near the truth to say that deep down she herself suspected this and hence her constant anxiety and constant recourse to confessors.

Significant in this context is her reserve in regard to St John of the Cross. Was she incapable of understanding his spirituality? From her 'judgment' on his commentary on the words 'seek thyself in me' it would seem so. Not only that, she does not include him in the array of confessors she so generously lauds. (*Relation* IV). True there are a couple of letters in his praise as a confessor addressed to his friend Ana of Jesus but they are of doubtful authenticity and not convincing simply because though she had got him for the community confessor when she was Prioress of the Incarnation, she herself had another priest as her director (letter to Gaspar de Salazar 13 Feb. 1573). She could not but recognise his goodness but she was afraid of his teaching. And was he not wary of her spirituality, or rather, of the harmful influence her way might have on others less spiritual than herself? Had he not this in mind in his painstaking destruction of visions, locutions and so on? Teresa was shrewd enough to guess but never consciously recognised that John, unlike the other confessors whom she quietly dominated, would not be impressed by the marvellous.

Yet how magnificently she trod her painful path! What saint more than Teresa gives us a sense of the glowing reality of God and the absoluteness of his claims. Surrender, love, humility; she knows to her heart what she is talking about and it rings with an irresistible force. Hers was a deeper prayer than she knew and it was by this that she lived. In its abandonment and living union, it is a prayer all of us are called to—a prayer of letting Jesus *be*. Because from the depths of heart she was humble and surrendered, the illusions did not matter. Her real life went on in all its truth and depth. However, though she lived truly she theorised falsely. She reveals the paucity of her theological knowledge: her ideas on mortal sin, her ignorance of the body-soul reality and humanness, expressed in the claim that to eat and sleep were agony; and note what she says about relatives (*Way* IX) and how, in fact, she acted. Unfortunately her daughters and others often go blindly by her theorising.

Yes, real dangers beset us on this island. One arises, of

course, from its sheer bleakness. To sustain this for a very long time without seeking refuge in some compensation will demand more than ordinary generosity and trust in God. But there is something else. We are not to suppose that in every case, or perhaps even in the majority of cases, the suffering of this state will be continually deepening or even remain at the same intensity; there will be times of respite. Whilst God is touching or pressing, we are bound to suffer, but he will refrain for a while, leaving us to develop what has been given and become accustomed to our new capacity. It is not unlikely that this respite will have all the refreshment of a flowery plateau one comes across of a sudden after a hard and bruising climb. Bearing in mind what has been said about 'favours', the psychological overflow and their relation to temperament, environment, expectancy, we can presume that something of the kind will happen in some cases — something akin to Teresa's prayer of quiet. Or it may be an awareness of progress; there may be a conviction of closeness to God and a general sense of well-being and happiness. It is good for us to be here! Hence the danger: 'Let me sit down and enjoy what I have. I have come a long way and given much; his demands will rise and I may not be able to meet them. I have met them so far and this is good enough'. So we sit down on the flowery plateau with our back to God, refusing the conditions of life for the second island.

God bears with us patiently, goes on taking the will to himself at prayer for he is not quick to desist from giving. Some, after a long, long time move on but many, alas, go back to the bridge over the first island. Outwardly there can seem to be heroism, utter fidelity to duty, heroic acceptance of suffering, severe penance, but these are escapes from God, from the real demand of God, which is to surrender more and more of spiritual possessions and powers. It all revolves around poverty, a veritable cliché these days but almost never understood in practice. It is the greatest possible self-denial and we do not want to understand it. 'Is that all there is to holiness', we say; 'I just can't believe it, no thank you, I want something more sublime than that'. So we camp in the valleys. It should be noted that, contrary to general opinion, it is when God has moved away, so to speak, that 'favours' happen. The almost universal mistake is to consider these as the divine presence and the troublesome aridity as his absence. Some will never know these valleys and so are saved the choice of passing them by for God. This is where John's uncompromising teaching comes in. He tells us that there is scarcely anyone who has not suffered heavy losses through clinging to these spiritual impressions, wanting them, seeking them. Many people imagine they *are* the spiritual life and so want them. Hardly a writer on the subject who does not say as much in one way or another.

The times of respite which, as we have seen, can hold danger for us when the psyche reacts with an upsurge of joyous energy and delight, are received in another way by others. John speaks of it (*Dark Night* 2, XII). It is a subtle but very real experience of dissatisfaction. How strange! In bitter pain we have longed for some easement, some glimmer of human happiness, and when it comes, though it be but a glimmer, we feel in a deep way that we have lost something we know not what. The experience of easement seems futile and empty. In fact, we are ill at ease. Below the level of consciousness we *know* that our pain is the effect of God's closeness; we know it when the pain is withdrawn. We know we have lost for a time that profound companionship which was there in our pain. Such a one as this is more at home in suffering, and it may well be God's providence for them that the night be rarely broken, perhaps only to help them to appreciate its meaning. In suffering they are aware, though not in an emotionally satisfying way which would neutralise the pain, that they are more in the truth, closer to reality and thus to God. They prefer to feel the utter emptiness of everything, the desolation and futility of life, rather than be fed with what is not him. This will be so until God unites them wholly to himself on the third island. This experience must be carefully distinguished from the cult of suffering referred to earlier, when suffering became spiritual riches, and also to the desire for penance and suffering as an escape from the exposure to love. Here it is the very exposure to love that is desired and the respite is known to be less of an exposure. It is not pain that is coveted but God's nearness.

There is likely to be a temptation to severe penance or the 'heroic' in some form. Here we are under the pressure of love. We need not feel this love, it will be there at a level below consciousness, and there will be a subtle urge to escape from the helplessness of love — of just receiving love and being unable to do anything in return. A desperate need will be felt to do something, to prove one's love. This has nothing to do with the earlier temptation towards ostentation, the desire to feel and be thought of as a spiritual, advanced person; this is a genuine thing, a cry from the depths of humanness to love on equal terms. Yet this can never be so with God. God is God and must be God, and we must let him be God, realising that our only way of repaying love is by letting ourselves be loved. For us, to love is to let ourselves be loved. This is hard for human pride. I think this is the explanation of the many extravagant penances you get in the mystics but it is significant that sooner or later they came to a realisation that these were valueless. The greatest penance is to go on accepting love, to allow oneself to be crushed by it even to the point of seeming no longer human.

In his explanation of his drawing of the mount, John of the Cross tells us that those who follow the winding path of spiritual riches arrive eventually but late. Too easily we adopt the

attitude that so long as we get there in the end this is all that
matters; the delays are of no consequence. That is to put the
whole thing outside the context of love. A loving heart could
never talk thus. For her, delay, hesitation, frivolity are of the
deepest concern. Is it nothing for a wife to play fast and loose
with her husband's love because she is quite certain he will
never throw her over? This is what we are doing when we are
careless and ungenerous. Surely the only real joy on earth as in
heaven is to give joy to God, or rather to be a joy to God. Both
Teresa and John observe that for someone in this state to be
hindered is of more moment to God because a greater loss to
the church than the failures of many less advanced. They
maintain that we can expect all hell to wage war against us to
prevent our entry into the last island where we will be safe for
ever. Teresa gives us moving pages about her own infidelity,
her struggles and final surrender.

She tells us that about the age of twenty God gave her what
she would term the grace of union (*Life* IV). In our scheme,
God gratuitously put her on the second island. It seems that, in
his visitations, God always pushes us a little further than we are
really capable of going, simply because he wants us to stretch.
Teresa failed to stretch, failed to affirm the grace that was
given her. She began to glimpse what it would mean to have
nothing but God, and the knowledge was too much for her:
long, dull hours at prayer, the boredom of a recollected life
. . . she preferred and chose the pleasant diversion of the
parlour. Fitted to live on the second island she chose to live on
the first island and so was utterly unhappy, divided, torn. For
long, long years she was back and forth upon the bridge; for
God was always drawing her along. There were times of
greater generosity when she reached its shores and stayed for a
while, but this did not last and back she would slither, only to
return again. All the same there was painful, intermittent

growth until the time came when face to face as never before with the implications of the passion of Jesus (*Life* IX) she made the renunciations he was pressing her to make, entered the second island, and pursued a resolute course across it. Here, in spite of sufferings and difficulties, she was happy. The misery of her divided life was over.

8

THE FURTHEST SHORE

No one can adequately describe how deep, how searching, how total must be a person's purification as God works to weld her to himself. Will we be able to detect one in whom this purification is far advanced? I do not think so, necessarily. It will need a deeply discerning heart to take her soundings, to catch the resonance of true humility, which never indulges in clichés, never plays the role of the humble one. She remains herself and says what she thinks, and acts before God and men as she really is, not trying to impress herself or others. Anyone looking for a stereotyped pattern of humility will not find it here. Listen to the person herself, listen beyond what one sees and hears, listen to the heart and you will know she thinks nothing of herself. Not only that, she is accepting her nothingness and making no fuss about it. She makes no fuss about her faults either, no exaggerated regrets. She is now too simple. She sees things as they are. This is the effect of the light in which she has accepted to live for so many long years. Self-satisfaction is literally impossible when this light shines. What God does in us, his living touch, always produces humility, ipso facto. No question of being on one's guard and carefully avoiding complacency. Complacency is quite impossible. Everything that comes from the self, as was said earlier, tends to pride.

Another sure note of one who has progressed far upon the second island is her intentness on God, her directedness. She is like an arrow speeding to the mark and nothing and no one can turn her aside. She may not be conscious of this directedness for it certainly does not mean that she thinks of nothing but God from morning to night. She may well have no awareness of God, or that she is serving him. She has grasped in a living way that 'without me you can do nothing' and that all her endeavour, attention, energy must be directed towards keeping herself available to Jesus, clinging to him, never letting him out of her sight, so to speak, so that he can do what he likes with her and in her.

But what of suffering? Must we find evidence of great suffering in one who is far across the island? This is a difficult question, and yet I think of practical import, and so we must try to find some sort of answer. Already something has been said of the caution needed in assessing the value of suffering, but more must be added, for this stage corresponds to what John calls the passive night of spirit, that horrible night wherein we go down alive into hell (*Dark Night* 2, vi). These words are enough to frighten anybody off. On the other hand, they can lead to a lot of nonsense.

I suppose we all have a general idea of what we mean by 'suffering'. It covers a wide, inescapable area of human experience, touching every life. Whilst we may have witnessed how often it has an ennobling, humanising effect, this is by no means always so; it can equally well have the reverse, which is to say that of itself it has neither. It is the human response which counts, what we do with suffering. Carried into the spiritual life it is no different. That one person seems to suffer more than another is not an indication that she is any holier, nor can we say that she has the greater chance of holiness. On the contrary, as we have seen, suffering can prove a snare. We can take pleasure in being a sufferer, it can boost our ego. At the outset, therefore, we must insist that it is a mistake to think that extreme suffering — using that word in its usual sense, covering the experiences we generally have in mind — is essential to total union with God. What is essential is the death of the ego, because this is the reverse side of our union with God. The inescapable (if we would attain this union) and truly mystical suffering is the mortal wounding of the ego, and I could well imagine this taking place, perhaps more effectively, where great suffering, in the ordinary sense, is absent. The real thing is likely to operate in an unobtrusive way, hidden behind what seem purely natural factors. The mortal wounding of the ego! A mere word until it is experienced. This is the 'terrible kenosis' referred to in the last chapter. We must not underestimate it, but at the same time we cannot describe it. We must leave it in its obscurity. We must accept to become a child, accept to be poor and wretched . . . one could go on, a mere string of nice words until the reality is demanded, and from nothing do we so shrink. I can well imagine someone well across this second island feeling that nothing ever happens to her — nothing interesting in the way of either favours or sufferings; everything so ordinary, so earthy, so banal.

Both John and Teresa testify to a period of most intense suffering just before a person's entrance into the third island. Must this be so? I hesitate to say. As far as we know, few have actually attained the third island, and fewer still have left accounts of their experience. Looking at Thérèse there does not seem evidence of it. We must discount her illness which, after all, happens to many others, and together with her trial of faith, this followed, not preceded her entry into the state of transforming union. Throughout her course, her sufferings were non-dramatic, uninteresting and seemed to remain so. What have Claire and Petra to say?

Claire has never experienced anything in the way of 'abandonment by God' which John would seem to indicate as the supreme suffering of this state. What is more, she says she has never really suffered. She says this with the utmost sincerity, and yet, knowing her as I do, I can say that purely objectively this is not true, but then suffering is never purely objective. I know she has for long years undergone most grievous trials which all but destroyed her health, and as she herself admitted, brought her close to death. However, the 'vision' of God, the certainty that he allowed this suffering, changed the character of it. She was happy, intensely happy in this suffering. A paradox, but I think most of us will have a glimmer of how this would be so. Julian of Norwich says something to the effect that if a man was aware of how closely God held him, then he might walk on the seabed and no harm come to him in soul or body. All the same, there is abundant evidence that Claire was smelted as iron in the fire, and for long years.

She felt that God wanted her in a state of life which would give scope, so to speak, for what it seemed he was working in her. It seemed that she must abandon herself entirely to prayer; that she was called to remain before God day and night in the most absolute way, and yet obedience kept her in a situation of constant activity. She was teaching. The effort to do this well, to fulfil all the demands made upon her, meant that she must 'resist' wellnigh irresistible calls to prayer. For some time before her entry into the third island her prayer was almost continually ecstatic and the effort to 'keep God at bay' in order to fulfil his will in the duties laid upon her ruined her health. What is more, the ecstatic state provoked contempt and ridicule. She did not mind this for herself so much as because she felt she 'let God down'. She saw no way of resolving this riddle, overcoming this impasse — God calling her in two directions at once. Her abandonment to the pain and the mystery of it is what she considers that culmination of surrender God asks before taking someone to himself. He had already taken her before he solved her dilemma. Of a sudden, the way became clear; she was freed to seek her true vocation, which proved to be eremitical. It must be noted that she had given up all idea of this, thinking that God must will her to stay in the active life; God intervened and cleared the path for her. Yet Claire can never be a typical case. Her way is extraordinary, that of 'light on', and this, I am convinced, is rare.

As for Petra, she admits to very great long-drawn-out interior suffering, but she is as emphatic as Claire that of itself the severity signifies nothing. Hers is a self-torturing temperament and this surely accounts for much, as well as the fact that psychological flaws were brought to the surface and highlighted. Living in a contemplative monastery as she does all this was felt more acutely. Then, too, it seems she has relatively great capacity, 'born with her eyes open' as she puts it, seeing behind life's facade to its ugliness and grief. For years she felt she was psychologically ill and eventually sought professional help, but to no avail. This neurotic element in no way surprises me. It seems inevitable that psychic weaknesses and conflicts will be shown up in God's light so that they can be faced and resolved. God works on the whole person, and it is the whole that is purified and transformed. It is easy to see how natural factors may account for why one person suffers more acutely at this stage than others. It is the response to suffering that matters and in Petra's case the helpless, long-drawn-out anguish, no matter what its cause, forced her into God's arms. There was no alternative. When trust was total, her problems fell off like a snake-skin. Neurosis is essentially a clinging to self.

When we realise that here the last strongholds of the ego are being assaulted, it is impossible not to think that a person will suffer acutely. An all-pervading awareness of ungodliness gives a feeling that God is far away and that it can never be otherwise. Her capacities have deepened immeasurably and these caverns cry out for God who alone can fill them. Nothing created can bring comfort and yet the soul does not possess God. She hangs between heaven and earth living in neither. This yearning for God can be intolerable but by no means unequivocal in identity. It may be experienced as sheer nausea for life, a dull, monotonous greyness. John has many moving passages describing the yearning passion of this wounded soul: a lioness searching for her stolen cubs, desperate, resistless; a dove pining for her mate, utterly forlorn and comfortless (*Dark Night* 2, XIII) (*Canticle* XXXIV, XXXV).

Petra says she suffered acutely all along the way. Did she experience more intense trials towards the end? Her answer was reserved. In one sense the suffering was less because her trust in God had grown. In another greater, because within the space of two years she was called upon to relinquish her last toe-holds on human happiness and security. But then, Claire was at hand. Not only did Petra find herself understood spiritually and reassured, but the whole of her was caught up in the love and delicate perceptiveness of this most womanly of women. Knowing something of this gift of love myself I can appreciate Petra's feelings. Petra wonders if without Claire she could have made the last surrenders which prepared her for entry into the third island; more positively, she realises that God sent Claire at this crucial moment of her life. She is letting me select from the notes and letters Claire wrote her. How beautiful, how revealing they are!

Prophetically Claire writes:

> God has achieved a surrender you neither saw nor understood. He has taken over at many levels and very deeply . . .

there is a plane of wholly divine initiative it has not yet pleased him — out of love — to achieve. Not time yet, though your longing and surrender will surely bring this time, 'so to say'.

I did not mean joy *in* suffering but joy in being allowed to suffer, to be conformed to Christ crucified. God has this gift still in store for you . . . you do know in one part of you that your suffering is redemptive, but one day he will tell you with the loving knowledge of what it means to be the Lamb of God . . . He makes me understand in your regard the words: 'they shall not break a bone of him'; he shows me that, though you are torn and bleeding — a lamb — yet not one of your bones has been broken. They are straight and beautiful.

Encouraging her to a total unselfishness in regard to a beloved person:

The will goes out to God until the time comes for transforming union. Then God must be the centre — he becomes the self, so the basic human constitution still stands. I feel this is where you are now. So what is just instinctive in you (natural self-centredness) is about, please God, to be transcended. You can do nothing but choose to love and be loved . . . I mean a decision to put X's good first and last and ignore your own. This is the test of your love and perhaps this choice of selflessness is what is still needed before God takes over in a way he has not yet done. Love and do what you will.

X's words about seeing death in relation to resurrection were so true. Our blessed Lord himself always spoke of them together, but not just because it would be unbearable otherwise, but because the two *are* one. The risen Jesus can only

rise from the dead. Your note speaks of the dreadfulness of
the human situation. Oh no, it would have been, but now
our Lord has transfigured it from within. We have truly
risen in him, and the deeper the human death, the more
profound the Christ-life. 'See my hands and my feet'. He
calls us to gaze on his wounds only because they are glorified.
Perhaps your watchword could be 'having joy set before him
he endured the cross'. With X too, the sharing in full will
come. All your sense of beauty will flow through you into
him. But the way there is the cross and maybe the joy won't
be in this life.

Understanding God's will in this, Petra surrendered even
though in bleakness and desolation. 'It's the only spark of
human happiness in my life', she moaned, but she gave, and
Claire helped her to maintain this selfless attitude. She was to
reap the fruit in this life. What she thought to be death-
dealing proved to be life-giving and the friendship she valued
so highly has been brought to perfect flowering and joy.

At the same time Petra was renouncing a position of
authority, a renunciation made many months before it came
into effect. This position had been a support, a legitimate
diversion, in that it forced her to think of others and mitigated
a little the severity of her interior suffering, even though it too
had become empty and meaningless. She had no assurance
from within herself that she could take life without it. She
could only trust in God. She made a total and effective renunciation in spite of the natural apprehension. She was over the
border when the actual time came, and Claire writes to her:

You know, don't you, how I shall be praying for you tomorrow — for that beautiful abandonment that he delights
to give you, and makes all fear of 'letting oneself down' seem

unworthy of him, not of our poor selves. How confident we can be, with God to rely on, and nothing human. So much grace will begin for you tomorrow, and however it hurts, we could not wish it otherwise, could we? Even for the littlest and poorest, there is a special poverty and littleness in being out of office, nothing can quite take its place. It is this that I think our God has lovingly ready for you, which is another way of saying, he will make you more like the Servant Jesus than was possible before.

Within these two years, Petra was faced with an operation which seemed to strike at the very roots of her womanhood. Claire entered into it as only a woman, and one who had understood and integrated the height, length, breadth and depth of the mystery of sexuality, could possibly do. Both of them saw the deep significance of what was asked and Claire expressed it:

> 'Do you accept', said he, 'the knife,
> Let me cut and give you life?
> Not higher heart or deeper breath,
> The body can but turn to death.
> But in your depths — a fountain sealed
> Ready now to be revealed.
> The knife will set its waters free
> To well up slow and silently
> To the pure silver of my sun'.
> 'Yes', she said, 'Be it done'.

No one could say that these troubles, of themselves, were worth writing home about. They belong to the common lot. But Petra saw God in them—ah, not in a way that 'sublimated' them, no, they were experienced in their earthy bitterness—

but she understood that this is how he comes. He asked her to abandon the last shreds of security, shreds that gave her some sort of meaning; asked her to look only to him for meaning and fulfilment. Ah, who can say how desolate she felt. She saw nothing ahead, no joy, nothing, nothing, nothing as far as she could see stretching for ever. And yet she went on telling God he was her all. She felt nothing.

But see the tender compassion and concern of God that he should send Claire to her—from the ends of the earth, literally. We are talking of God's transforming love and to speak of this friendship is no digression. Would that I could quote many more of Claire's letters but space does not permit. Clearly, it is no one-sided relationship. Claire feels that God has given her a friend in Petra: 'To be known after all these years—and to be loved and wanted—I can still hardly believe God has given it to me'. But to return to Petra, now standing on the further shore. She has said 'yes' as totally as is possible; she has surrendered as fully as she possibly can. One last instance faced her. Someone in whom she had great confidence seemed to question the genuineness of her spiritual life. The fact that it was all a misunderstanding did not take from the shock of its impact. She endured two days of emotional torture. There was nothing within herself to reassure her. Had she been mistaken? Was it that all those long years of unspeakable suffering need not have been? Had she taken the wrong turning? And yet at a deeper level she was at peace. Well, she was ready to start again. This very abandonment, in a secret way, showed her that, whatever appearances declared, she was in the right way, and that such a beginning is the end. She could be detached even from that way which had been 'no way'. She confided the anguish to Claire who made short work of it.

Standing on the further shore. But she does not know she is; she does not know where she is save in that deepest depth where there is only God. She knows only that she must go on, for he is not here, he is beyond. She comes to the bleak shore line with nothing to be seen beyond . . . nothing to be seen save the great expanse of cold, grey sea. No land in sight. She must not turn back, she cannot stand still, she must go on, must do what she cannot do for he is somewhere beyond, calling. She steps out to walk upon the waters, to go to him whom she cannot see. To do this is to be 'there' with him.

Or can we say she walks out upon the narrow promontory reaching far out to sea? She walks to the very tip, with the grey sea all around save for the narrow strip of land linking her to the island. The waves are slowly washing away the earth behind her, cutting her off. She could leap back to safer ground. She does not; she remains looking out to sea, looking at nothing else, waiting in hope. She is borne away to him.

9

THE THIRD ISLAND

This is the holy land, the kingdom of God where God is all in all. It was to bring us to this promised land that Jesus died. It is his own land, the land of his joy where he is wholly surrendered to his Father. In this land there is no need of sun or moon, for the Lord is its light.

The surrender of the second island, even at its furthest shore, is within the human compass, fortified, enlightened by God's mystical help. The next irretrievable step is God's alone. The person's consent to this specific thing cannot be given because it cannot be asked. What God does here is completely beyond her capacity to imagine or understand. Her consent has been given all along the way, an unconditional consent 'do with me what you will'. God can therefore act with total respect for his creature's freedom. Up to the present the person has given what she possessed, all the substance of her house, and only implicitly gave herself, but now it is specifically herself that is given or rather taken. Who can grasp what this means, the extent of this gift? It is death, but a death that is life, true life. The person is taken away from herself and that permanently. What will it be to live without a 'self', to exist as a wraithlike thing? Looked at from the purely human angle, terrible indeed, but not when it is the effect of God becoming all in all. This is perfect human fulfilment and heaven on earth.

Hitherto, God's union with us was temporary and partial, now it is permanent, total. Only now can we really speak of an indwelling. In essence it is a state of rapture, that is, the self taken out of the self and that abidingly. There is no counterpart in nature. It can be understood only in the incarnation. It derives from this and, as someone dared to suggest, can be called an extension of it. A person in this state is totally possessed by Jesus, identified with him in his surrender to his Father. Thus, through her, Jesus is on earth in an incomparable way. His kingdom has come in her and because of this comes even more fully into the world.

Up to now we have spoken of the person knowing, loving, surrendering; we can do so no longer, for being is identified with its activities: she *is* love, *is* surrender. In this sense we can say that faith is transcended. The mysteries of faith, which on the second island were entered into and became principles of living, are now simply Jesus. This happy creature is at last fully christian, fully human.

Just as we claimed for the second island, and the bridge leading to it, a completely new intervention of grace which cut it off absolutely from the first island in as much as a new dimension was introduced, so here: the third island is not a more advanced stage of the second, it comprises a wholly new mode of existence. What is more, whereas all across the expanse of the second island, return was possible — one of the 'functions' of the bridge — there is no return from the third. It is a definitive state. It is the end of the journey, the goal is reached, and yet it is only a beginning. The third island is limitless, embracing eternity. But here we must not speak of traversing it, as on the first and second islands, but entering ever more deeply into it. On the former island, even when surrender was complete as far as lay within our power, it was still 'I' surrendering to God, 'I' choosing God. But here there is no 'I' in that sense. In some mysterious way, God has replaced the self, the 'I'. De Caussade makes a fine and telling distinction. 'There is a time', he says, 'when the soul lives in God' (the second island) 'and a time when God lives in the soul' (third island). To avoid any notion of pantheism or loss of identity, we must return to the principle that the individuality, the distinction, the otherness of the creature is established in direct proportion to its nearness to the creator. The more surrendered to and possessed by God, the more immersed in God, the more the self is self. This individualisation at its highest peak means that there is no pattern of living on the third island. On the former islands there were patterns; to some extent one could generalise, but here hardly at all. Each inhabitant of this island is a world, a universe of her own. We can only listen to what each tries to tell us of her experience and see where other testimony agrees.

Must a person know she is in this state? Could she be there and not know it? It would seem that we must affirm that knowledge of it is essential. On the bridge, on the second island, we cannot really know where we are, but it is hard to think that when the work is accomplished, when there is perfect union, we would not know it in some way. What is more, though we can never go back, we can fail to go forward, and this is of great moment. To go forward, to penetrate more deeply into this land, to allow God to penetrate every pore of one's being, it is essential to know where one is so as to correspond with God. No one could doubt that St Teresa was quite certain where she was. Even if her writing on the seventh mansion were not proof enough, we have her affirmation in a letter (Nov 1581). Likewise, St John of the Cross's *Spiritual Canticle* from chapter xx and his *Living Flame* witness to his own personal experience. But both of these are in what we call the 'light on' category. What of 'light off'? What of St Thérèse? Most certainly she knew. She was quite certain she had reached the summits of the spiritual life. And considering the climate of her milieu and its identification of the state of mystical marriage with high-flown experiences as described in St John of the Cross, this is amazing. 'I asked God to accomplish in my soul all that I found described there' (*Novissima Verba* 31 Aug 1897). Thérèse knew nothing of his flamboyant experience but was unperturbed, serenely certain.

We are trying now to answer the question: 'What does someone know of this world-shattering experience? How does she know?' All of us can read what Teresa and John have to say and somehow, vaguely, just because they are 'light on' we recognise that of course they would know, for they would 'see', 'see' God in possession. Teresa expresses it in terms of a vision of the Trinity dwelling within her, and similarly John. As Claire belongs to this category, I asked her if she could say anything about her experience, how she knew she had passed into the state of transforming union. With great reserve she replied: 'Jesus has always been my music, but the music was all I noticed. I wasn't aware, before, that it was in some way "I" who played, or "I" who was the organ. But after he brought me to the third island, I found the difference. He was now all. The music played of itself—there was *only* the music. I was now living what had seemed my life before, but only seemed because I only looked at him and didn't advert to myself. Now myself has become him'.

Thérèse in her darkness, how did she know? Was that experience of the 'dart of love' God's way of affirming what her heart surmised? Or was the testimony of her sister Mother Agnes the outward witness to her deepest conviction? Undoubtedly Mother Agnes thought her a saint—though probably for the wrong reasons—and Thérèse had fantastic trust in her Was this seemingly lowly way of assurance God's beautiful way with Thérèse, all of a pattern with her lovely lowliness? But what is quite certain is that Thérèse could never have believed Mother Agnes unless she knew in her depths that it was true. It is my experience that we can only hear what we already know. Anything completely extraneous leaves us untouched, but an outward voice, affirming a secret knowledge, how powerful an awakening this can be!

It will be useful here to look at Petra. I quote from a letter to Claire:

It was my 'hermit day' and I had an extraordinary sense of peace, as though nothing could ever touch me again. This peace had been growing for some weeks but, being occupied with the community and other things, I hadn't stopped to taste it. This day, completely free from everything, it flooded into my consciousness and wrapped me round. I was in the garden, and for a moment I seemed to be looking within and I saw or realised in a mysterious way that *I* was not there. There was no 'I'. I can't say more than that. *I* had gone. It wasn't that I saw or felt God, but it was as if I were in a vast and lonely plain far removed from everything. For a few weeks I lived to some extent outside myself, by which I mean only a very small part of me seemed in contact with what was going on around me. I had similar experiences of this estrangement in earlier days but they were extremely bitter. This was bewildering joy. I felt physically and nervously exhausted but I managed to carry on, and I do not think anyone saw anything was different with me. I longed to tell you and then I decided against it. If what I believed was really true, then with your usual insight you would know it without my saying it and this would be a confirmation. So when we met I said nothing. We were discussing the man-

sions and the state of union. I said as casually as I could that
I thought de Caussade had something to say when he spoke
of the soul living in God and God living in the soul. There
was silence. You felt ill and suggested we walked in the fresh
air. Still you made no comment. But next day you wrote to
me telling me that, when I said those words you saw what
had happened and were overwhelmed. This confirmation
was precious to me. 'You have given me more joy than I ever
expected would be mine, because I see you wholly his'.

Well, this state of bewildered happiness lasted a couple of
weeks, and then I found myself in the wasteland. But the
sense of estrangement continued to some extent and is with
me still. I know that, in reality, I have died . . .

Later bewildered in her new state, she wrote of her pain to
Claire, who replied:

This is really what joy means, isn't it? Nothing but God —
and God apparently not there . . . so that the whole soul
is gift, is surrender, is that 'lived nothingness' we spoke of.
When I said that you were conscious of yourself, this is what
I meant: that your experience is of *what you are*, that is,
an emptiness God has filled. But you are never shown the
fulness, God, the sole reason for your being emptied — all
you see is the creature side. You call it 'blind will that clings,
or rather, is held'. If you could see the holding, you would
forget all the anguish of being that blind, subhuman thing
— all would vanish in the light of the Holy One to whom the
will is soldered. I don't think, given this experimental darkness, which is mystical light and hence unseen, that you
would ever be able, in full confidence, to believe in his
having taken possession. That was why I once suggested you
should write it down. I knew the days were coming when the
sheer weight of darkness would make what your heart told

you a mockery. But you know it is not. You know at a depth deeper than any darkness, a depth the 'darkness cannot overcome' that God has made you his. Are *you* paying the price? Is it not Jesus, as you gropingly wonder? To know the full smallness, the incompleteness of being human, to open wholly to the suffering and frustration and endless pettiness of living: it is Jesus who knows that, who is living it in you and living it in radiant happiness. Secretly you know this, you know the weariness and pain is the shadow that tells you he is there. His sacramental signs . . .

Later Petra was to write:

You remember, Claire, when we were together and I told you how convinced I was that your experience was authentic, convinced that you were possessed by God, and you said that it was such a comfort to receive this assurance and then added that it could be done without? Well, it is like that with me. If you were to tell me that I was mistaken, that God had not 'taken over', I would want to believe you because I feel you speak from God and I want to hear all he wants to tell me, but it would be impossible. Trying to imagine what I would do if you or another whom I thought spoke from God, told me I was deluded, I could only fall back on two absolutes: the infinite love of God and my total poverty. There is nothing else to it, and if God has not filled my poverty, then there is no meaning to me. Nothing makes sense. There is nothing whatever I could do about it. Formerly I could 'make up my mind' to give God everything, to do whatever he asks. That is what I used to do even though our Lord took good care to show me that *I* could not do. Even so, I could still hold on, still cling; that basic 'I will' was still there. Now it seems as if it isn't. That way of thinking makes no sense now. If I was helpless before, it is nothing to

what I am now. You know, if I were face to face with a trial,
I could no longer fall back on self, steel myself, make up my
mind to accept and suffer. Now I can only receive what I am
given. I know I cannot choose anything against God's will,
but on the other hand 'I' cannot face, bear and so on.

I am certain that in all that matters he will never let me
fail, in spite of what I feel he would move me always to
please him, but in areas of non-importance, he is likely to
leave me to my native weakness. But the point I am really
making is that, though there is no seeing or feeling of God
and his love and that he is pleased with me, there is a profound certainty. I can only think that it is God's affirmation
of himself because it does not come from me. I think your
expression 'luminous darkness' is perfect.

There is more to be drawn from this correspondence between
friends but I would like to stop and consider some of the points
Petra has revealed. There, clearly, is the certitude. It seems
that it comes from within, but yet needs or has needed outside
affirmation. By God's providence it came through Claire
whose experience is of 'light on'. Earlier I made the point that
this charism is given for others. Here we have an instance of it.
Claire is able to 'see' God in Petra in a way Petra cannot see
herself. Petra expresses her wonderment at the providence of
God:

How often I marvel at the loving providence that brought
you into my life just when I needed you; what a proof that
he never lets us down; that he always gives us what we need.
It seems to me almost essential for one in this state to have
someone who understands. I am speaking for the 'light off'
experience. I suppose that what we are looking for from one
who understands is to be told that what one is saying is in

perfect harmony with what one is. Many, many times I have wanted to be with you just because I am certain you would detect in me untruth, any discrepancy between what I say or don't say and what I am.

Petra had some sort of initial 'light on' experience. Was it a 'light on'? I asked her about it. She said that, compared with all that has followed it was 'light on', but of a negative nature, if that is not a contradiction. Her point seems to be that it was not God she saw, she saw emptiness, saw that self had gone. That experience has never been recaptured in so vivid a way. This seems a far cry from Teresa's vision of the glorious Christ celebrating his nuptials with her and yet have we any reason to doubt that it is fundamentally the same grace? Basically it is the fulfilment of our Lord's words, 'If anyone loves me he will keep my word and my Father will love him, and we will come to him and make our abode with him'. Those for whom the light is on, as with Claire and St Teresa, have a glimpse of this hidden reality. The basic difference is that the one sees it from God's side, sees God at work, the other sees it from the human, sees the consequent emptiness. The first state is rare; it is the second that is normal and that is why I must say more about it. Those rare souls in the 'light on' state will not need this book, it is those in the 'light off' category that need help, very little in this state, but some nevertheless, as Petra has testified.

The experience of lowliness and emptiness consequent on this sublime state must be emphasised. Let us listen to Petra again:

Your letter, with its comfort, was very timely. My long silence has been due in great part to lack of time, sufficient, uninterrupted, relaxed time for writing a deeply personal letter, but partly because I have been so bruised and weary that, when I sat down to write, my spirit failed me. Your letter, with its uncanny insight, seemed to break down whatever was making me inarticulate. No, it is not doubt that plagues me; your letter only confirms what my heart knows but it means so much, in bewildering obscurity, to have another's voice affirming. No, no, I never expected that there is a short-cut that by-passes the drudgery of human experience. I don't want one, I want to drink to the dregs the chalice of my Lord. In my case (and isn't this the common, ordinary state?) how non-glamorous, ignoble this chalice! What does it amount to with me? A sense of inner fragility and faintness, which taps, knocks at the wall of my body too. I seem unable to face up to any pressure. I feel faced with an immense 'trial' utterly beyond myself, and yet when I look, where is the trial? What have I to suffer compared with so many people? I have good health, am surrounded with love, have everything I need, and yet life itself seems more than I can bear—the unutterable loneliness and emptiness, the mystery and obscurity. Yesterday, I heard of a poor woman enduring humiliating helplessness for ten years, and now, faced with new symptoms, her splendid spirit is breaking and she can take no more. Just one of millions similarly suffering from seemingly unbearable afflictions. And what relation has my life to hers? By comparison I have nothing to suffer. It is my hope that this 'suffering' of mine which is nameless, which really has no right to be called suffering, this inner 'dissolution' should be a way through which Jesus comes to others in their grief and pain. I feel overwhelmed with everything: with the beauty of the world, with its terrible pain, with its evil and ugliness, the devilish brutality of man to man—with the Word of God so mighty and so obscure. I could weep my eyes out with—I don't know what! Oh, how fragile I am, without achievement; no human victory, no human beauty, only that which is he, who experienced in all its raw bitterness the human condition.

Occasionally I am overwhelmed by emotional turmoil, tumultuous feelings of disgust and revolt. I seem swept off my feet by what I cannot control. It could be frightening, indeed it is frightening, and yet sheer experience shows me that I am safe, that the crashing waves of temptation break harmlessly against the walls of my citadel. 'Crashing waves of temptation', what grandiose words for the petty things I mean: an arrangement that upsets me, the feeling of being a powerless member of a group, without rights of privacy, the pressure of community life on a very independent woman, who is not by nature a community woman — all the nothings that go to make the grinding routine of religious life or any life. Of course, my temperament has a lot to do with this, others wouldn't react so strongly or be in such a degree conscious of the 'tears of things'. But my heart tells me the Lord is in it; this lowly way is his way. In the sight of men I seem to fail — but in God's eyes? I ask to tread no other path. I am content to feel these difficulties to the end of my life. He has taught me, and still teaches me the human can't which becomes his glorious *fiat*.

And again:

Your letter was moving in its truth. 'What God has done lasts — lasts and constantly grows deeper — but we become as it were acclimatised to his heights, and the sense of happy strangeness disappears as though it had never been'. That happy strangeness, the 'strange islands' of St John of the Cross, that sort of timelessness when we see to our depths that God has taken us a decisive step forward and that nothing can be the same again! Ah, that experience, as you say, can only be passing. 'To rise above the true stuff of human living would be to disavow Jesus who learnt obedience through what he suffered and suffered to the end'. I feel this, Claire, I know this is true.

'Unimportance', yes, Claire, I feel that is the best word to express a vital point. 'Littleness', 'helplessness', 'poverty' can be run to death and lose their life. 'Non-importance'carries with it a dreadful awareness of one's basic insecurity and meaninglessness. It's not only a question of being non-important in one's community, business and so on, it is on the cosmic level also. Isn't this one of the frightening experiences of us moderns — the unimportance, the vulnerability and fragility of man? It might seem that we christians who are striving to live out what we believe, who see our meaning in God, who know, in faith, the grandeur and security of man in God, can let go this craving for importance. Oh, but we can't. We carry on the pursuit in a far more subtle and dangerous way. We want spiritual importance. We want our interior life, our way to God, to have elements which make us feel important. We want to rise above the mediocrity of the common lot. This might seem justifiable but in reality it could mean nothing but a desire for a more interesting form of spiritual life, a desire to escape from the sheer drabness of the ordinary, seeking a short-cut from the drudgery . . . back again to that secret coveting of spiritual riches, beauty, glory, achievement.

To be unimportant as a child — seemingly so simple, it is the hardest thing a human being can do, to accept that it depends utterly on God, to let go its petty, sham securities, to abandon itself unreservedly in darkness and pain, in light and joy, it matters not, to God. For this, Jesus lived and died, and this is the substance of his work in us in all that befalls.

How different this lowly admission from the ideas usually formed of the state of transforming union and which mystical writers seem to affirm. For both Teresa and John the state is one of surpassing glory and delight. John would say that soul-suffering is no longer possible and our Lady's sufferings were a special dispensation. The soul has a burning desire for the salvation of souls, for martyrdom, prepared to lay down a thousand lives, to be humiliated and scorned. Everything is in terms of grandeur, glory, heroism, far removed from the common experience.

But even should the witness of these great mystics really be against what Petra claims (and this book stands by her), we need not worry. We look to Jesus. Here is one wholly possessed by God and what do we see? Where is the 'sublime', the 'heroic' in this precious life? Here was a man tempted as we are but without sin. His dear mother, was she spared the sufferings of our human lot? Have we any grounds for thinking so? This distraught mother searching for her lost child knowing the searing pain of not understanding him, seeing him growing away; the bewildered little woman standing on the edge of the crowd trying to get to him, unable to grasp what was going on. The gospel of John shows her standing at the foot of the cross. Whether or not this was historically true is beside the point. She was there in spirit, surrendered to God in a mystery too great for her. Like us, she chose to stand at the foot of the cross, sharing in his sacrifice, accepting the bitter experience of human existence.

Claire reflects to Petra:

I keep thinking of our dear Lady—a peasant girl in a small backward land. How absolutely God trusted himself and all his dear ones to her. I suppose her special quality was the same thing grace is always seeking to produce in us—a perfect focus on God, on being there for him to possess us, with no uncommitted areas. Yet since this is a focus on God, on being there for him to possess us, not us him, then the human experience of this intensity of concentration would be just the opposite of what would be expected. It would have to feel like diffusion, non-possession, wouldn't it? The very blur of the experience is the proof of its non-natural origin. I wonder how much she suffered from the dark certainty she must have lived in from very early on?

Little Thérèse grasped this so well. She deliberately and persistently rejected the attempts of her sisters to force her into the role of 'saintliness'. She knew God had made her holy, but she refused to play the role of the saint. There was no admitting to fine sentiments she did not feel, rather she let it be known that she felt the same as everyone else. Encouraged to say a few edifying words to the doctor — words from the lips of a dying 'saint' — she refused; the doctor must think as he likes. One has only to read the unabridged version of *Novissima Verba* to see how Thérèse was misunderstood. It is just not true to say her message in no way suffered through the editing and expurgating of her writings and sayings. We see a careful elimination of any word or deed that did not conform to the accepted standard of holiness. But we need to know that when undergoing painful treatment on her already agonising body, her cries of pain were heard throughout the cloisters; that when she had to be lifted out of bed she asked for a particular sister who, strong as she was, could lift her and hold her with the minimum of pain; that her sensibilities wounded she fell into a 'mood' which she could not shake off for a whole day . . . Thérèse did not want these things hidden. She was crying out that Jesus was her holiness, that all that pleased him in her was to see her love her nothingness, see the utter trust she had in him. How few have understood Thérèse! Some have succumbed to her child-like charm, her smile, her roses; others have rejected this as sentimentality — a spoilt child, all the limitations of a provincial girl, self-occupied, immature: God can't do much with that. But it is precisely *that* with which he deals as with all of us. Others see her as heroic, a genius, a seraph. 'I have only trusted God and accepted to be little' persists Thérèse.

Our cowardice and our pride are past-masters at disposing of the saints. We don't burn them: we put them on a pedestal, which is the same thing as putting them on the shelf. They do not challenge us any more. They are no longer men and women just like ourselves, flesh, blood, nerves; somehow they are quite special, they have been given what we have not. They did not really spring from our common stock. This flower of holiness is not of our soil. Those far above us do not challenge us, it is the one close to us who does what we do not do, becomes what we do not become, this is whom we fear, this is the one we must dispose of. What is more, we find vicarious satisfaction in seeing one of ourselves raised to a superhuman state. We like to think that this is what human nature really is. The saints never felt beautiful and sublime.

Look how we have coped with St Teresa, our dazzling, seraphic mother. Not one of her daughters would presume to think she could become what she is. Yet Teresa had no greater advantage than the rest of us. We are ready to acknowledge her human qualities, how down-to-earth she was, a true woman; we are ready to acknowledge the foibles and weaknesses which make her lovable, but further than that, no. If we would strip her of her cloth of gold and glittering mask, what would we find? One without beauty, without majesty, like her Lord. But the sight is too painful, too ugly, it speaks of things we do not wish to hear.

I think God was at his wits' end when he gave us Thérèse.

'Well, they won't be able to put her on a pedestal, this little one'. But we did. How cleverly we evaded her stark, obstinate declaration of the true nature of sanctity, which is the destruction of human pride. She was among us as a burning, shining light. But the light streaming from this little one was too searching, too shattering. We preferred darkness to such light. She was true to the end. Those who admired her and thought her a saint hoped she would die 'like a saint' in an 'ecstasy of love'. I shall die of love, like Jesus on the cross. We reject the saints because we reject our Lord himself.

Those in the third island are identified with Jesus. He surrenders to the Father in them and each of their lives is sealed with his. As John of the Cross says, they enter deeper and deeper into the caverns of Christ, into an understanding of his incarnation, death and resurrection — not a notional understanding but an immersion in these very mysteries. Now the sacraments come into their own. That which formerly could be received only partially, now meets with no obstacle. The unutterably 'alien' and 'other', God himself, meets in the soul a life 'other' to its depths. The sacramental encounter is continuous. Two abysses meet and know one another. Every reception of the sacraments means a deeper surrender and possession by God and always it is in the church and for the church.

Petra, for all her darkness, realises this presence of Jesus. Asked if there were any differences between her present trials and those she experienced earlier, she was emphatic that there is all the difference in the world, though in fact they are made of the same stuff. If one gave the name of 'suffering' to what went before, then one must find another name for this. Formerly she suffered 'without God', in a sense — she was not united to him, she was distanced from him — but now, if she stops to reflect, she sees that she is always conscious of possession yet without being conscious of it! She knows God is always with her. What is more, she is able, from her experience, to say simply that it is Jesus who suffers in her. Is this the meaning behind John's statement that the transformed soul does not suffer? Can this be called suffering? Profound happiness is the vibrant note of all who tell us of their experience, happiness in suffering, happiness in 'unhappiness'. 'I have reached the stage when I can no longer suffer because all suffering has become sweet to me'. There is no self-interest; God's good pleasure is all that matters.

> Your vocation to poverty (writes Claire to Petra) fills me with holy awe . . . how utterly destructive it is of what human pride regards as self-evident if it is to be a saint. It is all very well to speak of 'self-dissatisfaction' but oh, in practice, what it means of trust in God and an acceptance of the truth. No comforting evasions here — not even the happy glow of knowing one is all one would wish — not even wishing really, except for him to have the pleasure. It is impossible to live this utter destitution except in Jesus . . . your very state of accepted 'nothingness' is the radiant proof that you are his. It is mystical in the strictest sense. No one would even *know* it pleased God unless Jesus revealed it from within.

Petra has a profound grasp that her stark, human experience is mystical, that it is, in fact, Jesus living it in her. 'Son of God though he was, he learned obedience through what he suffered'. Was not this school of suffering precisely the experience of what it means to be a man and to die, to be born dying? No one has ever plumbed the depths of human littleness and wretchedness as he did; no one ever tasted the bitter draught of human poverty as he. His very sinlessness heightened the awareness of this poverty. Yet Jesus never evaded it, he lived it out fully to the inevitable end, death. We see him in a world which bewildered him. 'A stranger and afraid/ In a world I

never made'. True he seems at home in the material creation,
for his pure spirit saw it as it really is, a revelation of God. But
the world of men! How it must have bruised him! Even his
mother's innocent obtuseness came as a shock. The little
boy cried in amazement 'But why were you looking for me?
Didn't you realise I would be here?' He lived with the holiest
man and woman and nothing in them could grieve him,
but what of the other children and grown-ups round about?
Growing with his growth was a passion of love for God his
Father. He, we must presume, 'saw'. What when he came
up against human indifference, man's frivolity and irres-
ponsibility in the face of life, his untruth, his evasions?
These must have wrung his heart even as a child. The gospels
give us glimpses of this grief throughout his public life, a grief
that was a bewilderment, 'how could men be so blind, so
untrusting, so lacking in faith and seriousness, even the best of
them?'

Was he spared the experience of feelings of resentment,
irritation? Why should we think so? These are not sin, they are
part of our human condition; unsatisfied, at odds with our
surroundings, hardly knowing what is the matter with us. We
could easily draw from the gospels the impression that Jesus'
was a highly charged temperament, one relatively quickly
depleted. On the walk through Samaria, the disciples are fit
enough to go on to the village for food, he must rest, exhausted
as he is. Those outbursts against the stupidity of his disciples,
the perverseness of the pharisees; nerves stretched to breaking
point. Was it experience of this kind as well as others beyond
our ken that drew from him that spontaneous repudiation:
'Why do you call me good? One is good, God' (Mk 10:18). Oh
holy Jesus, you became one of us, shared our lot to the full.
You sat on our side of the border, clothed in our grime, tainted
with our foulness, eating our husks. Holy One, strong One,

beloved of the Father!

It could be objected that these reflections are personal, that in fact we do not know our Lord's experience. Be that as it may, the gospel and the epistle to the Hebrews give us two facts we cannot ignore: we see him prostrate, shuddering with horror, crying out to be saved from death; we hear him crying on the cross that his Father is not there any more.

Raised up on the cross Jesus becomes the revelation of what man truly is before God. 'On that day the pride of man shall be humbled' (Is 2:11). We see a being of unutterable, frightening dependency, suspended between heaven and earth, belonging to neither. There he was, exposed for all the world to see, like some poor beast skewered through. Helpless, humiliated, naked, his maleness displayed. Crucifixion, as historians tell us, was the most degrading of deaths; the poor human body at its humblest, its functions out of control. Truly this is man. Can we doubt it? And through it all the sweetness of his spirit, patient, worshipping, loving, forgiving, surrendering. God wills us to have imprinted on our christian souls this spectacle of human littleness and divine love. We say we love it; in reality we hate it and turn away. How truly the prophecy of Isaiah is fulfilled even to this day:

> Without beauty, without majesty we saw him, no looks to attract our eyes; a thing despised and rejected by men, a man of sorrows and familiar with suffering, a man to make people screen their faces, he was despised and we took no account of him (Is 53:2 — 4).

Set against this the human ideal of the Yogi — the Yogi only?

> He is then free from birth and death, from pain and sorrow and becomes immortal . . . his body, breath, senses, mind, reason and ego are all integrated in the object of his contemplation . . . . a state of supreme bliss.

Can we deny that secretly this is what we are wanting in our spiritual life, something resembling this, at any rate? Ingrained in us is this longing for a beautiful spiritual life, to be beautiful for God! Jesus shows us what is beautiful in God's eyes: the total acceptance of lowliness and the surrender of that lowliness to the Father's love. Jesus, by living it through to the end, carried it all to the Father. He delivered the pitiable human condition from meaninglessness, drew the fangs of suffering and death. All is changed now. Nothing is just what it seems to be. Outwardly it seems the same but it is a different reality. This is what it means to live the risen life of Jesus. It does not mean living in a euphoric or exalted state. Essentially it means letting God be God in us. Oh, how little is this understood even by those who think they understand it.

As we are still looking at Petra I must say that it would be a great mistake to think of her as a very suffering person. She is not. She just lives, or as it seems to her, just exists, rather like a little donkey. Half the time she doesn't know what she is like, what state she is in, whether she is suffering or not. The basic thing is her littleness and unimportance, and her surrender at every moment. Here we could quote St Teresa, speaking of 'a self-forgetfulness so complete that it really seems as though the soul no longer existed because it is such that she has neither knowledge nor remembrance that there is either heaven or life or honour for her, so entirely is she seeking the honour of God . . . so extreme is her longing for the will of God to be done in her that whatever his Majesty does she considers best: if he wills she should suffer, well and good; if not, she does not worry herself to death as she did before, (*Interior Castle*, VII mansion, 3). Petra is not aware that she is employed in seeking the honour of God nor does she feel extreme longing. When her state becomes just a little too donkey-like she turns to Claire for a word of assurance, and it always comes, a word fragrant with truth: 'yes, everything in your soul is *really* what he wants. He has searched the world, has searched history, to find souls who will accept to be nothing, who will let him be God. Jesus so fills your soul that all self-delight has died; you can only offer him, mutely, the sacrifice of all he asks. You die in him and so he lives in you'. Petra is a very happy person. From time to time also, the 'south wind' (cf *Spiritual Canticle* XVII) blows through her garden and the fragrance flows, aroused by a word from Claire or by some interior illumination which shows her obscurely the wonder of her union with Jesus and how tenderly the Father loves and cherishes her.

It would be a great mistake to imagine that because I have spoken of Petra's way and state as ordinary, the experience she describes is typical. No, as we said earlier, each person and each vocation is unique. Petra has her own vocation. I found it fascinating to listen to Claire and Petra when on a rare and happy occasion the three of us were together for the purpose of discussing this chapter of the book. They can say little and yet it is obvious that each understands what the other is saying. Struggling to give some account of their experience one of them referred to time. An interesting exchange followed; clearly each of them felt that time had changed its character for her:

'Time flows by, but I am not of it'.

'Time no longer threatens'.

'I am free of time'.

This seemed to have special meaning for Petra and she explained:

Looking back I see that nearly all my life and with growing intensity I have suffered from profound anxiety. The

anxiety was rooted in my relation to God. Not that I feared
his 'wrath' or anything like that, it was just a fear of existence, fear of the Other; anxiety as to how I stood to him;
only he mattered, was I loving him? Time, terrible time
was passing away . . . was I near to God? Briefly, I lacked
God and as life means nothing but him and time's only
worth was in bearing me to him, time was ambiguous and
threatening, threatening on all levels. When God suddenly,
unexpectedly, carried me to the third island, this anxiety
was extinguished. I possess him. Time has no meaning.

For Claire there was no marked, sudden change as with Petra,
but she feels now that all her potential is realised. She is as God
meant her to be. Petra speaks of 'as if I have died'; twice she
repeated this phrase but added 'not in the sense that I have
entered into a state of unalloyed bliss. But I know I have
crossed the great divide: somehow now I am on the other side
and physical death has no relevance in that sense. It has relevance, but not in that sense'.

Listening to these and other things, I was aware that both of
them were conscious of living in a wholly new dimension of
existence, unknown to the rest of us.

Petra is aware, more at some times than at others, that all
save a tiny portion of her is absorbed elsewhere. She is not
aware of what she is absorbed in, what she is knowing or
loving, she just knows that she is in some way being devoured.
She cannot get at this inner reality and never tries to. She is
content just to be; life passes by, passes over her; she feels,
reacts, can be hurt, cast down, groan under the pressure of
life, and in another sense be 'away', almost with a sense of non-
being which can frighten at times. Below the level of superficial doubts and questionings is an assurance, an inability to
worry or be anxious; no temptation 'to do something about it'

by way of rousing the attention, applying the mind, making an effort. She knows her business is to receive, to be moved, to be carried. It seems to her that her capacity is so filled as to leave scarcely room for other experiences; there is only sufficient attention and room for what she has to do in her daily round. Looking back now she sees this was in great part true of her long sojourn on the second island. It used to worry her somewhat realising that she was never wholly present to what she was doing. She used to think she was lacking in concentration and feel remiss. Now she understands what was happening. Again she used to worry because she seemed to have lost all feeling for beauty and other human interests. This caused her real suffering, creating a sense of isolation and bleakness. Now it is painless. Always she is aware of deep contentment. She knows she possesses God and having him has all things else. The tearing, the anxiety, the sense of terrible 'absence' are no more.

'My sole occupation is love'. St John of the Cross's affirmation is true. 'Prayer is my life' would be equally true. Taking prayer as what God does to us, his taking possession of us and our surrender to him, then it is impossible to confine it to one part of one's life or part of one's day. It is the day and the night too. It is what we were made for, it is what God meant human life to be — a total, constant reception of him. Is this what Jesus meant when he called himself the life? Jesus alone knows what prayer really is. Through him, prayer is life and prayer is Jesus — who brings God and man together.

Obviously our prayer, like his in his mortal life, cannot be lived only on one level. There seem to be three levels through which we move on our daily round.

The first we would call the prayer of activity, the kind of union we have when all or most of our attention must be concentrated on some task. The comparison that comes to mind is that of two lovers working together. The work occupies the forefront of their minds but each is deeply aware that the other beloved is with him. The whole nature of the activity is changed by this mutual presence. Let one go away and all is different.

But at times they will cease from work and talk together and this we could call the prayer of attention. It is the sort of prayer we have when our minds are engaged in some spiritual action: office, reading, meditation, spiritual conversation. We are looking at God but through natural concepts. Thus our lovers are conversing together in a direct way but the subject of their conversation occupies their attention as much as one another's presence. In this sort of prayer God is asking us to use our natural faculties for him, not to be silent, but there are times when he wants pure prayer.

Pure prayer we liken to 'just loving'; two lovers wrapped up in one another, unaware of anything else, occupied with love itself. But this passionate surrender can have varying intensities and varying degrees of conscious awareness. To change the image, this prayer is the emergence into full light of the great river of prayer running deeply and silently through the less absorbing forms of prayer, but on the surface of this mighty river there may float a myriad of sticks and leaves and bits of straw. These are wholly irrelevant; they are not the river nor do they in the least deter the river from its inexorable surge to the sea — rather, they are carried along with it. This flotsam is what we call 'distracting thoughts'. Clearly they are not worth thinking about! This is the living water Jesus promised would flow in us if we 'come to' him.

Unless every moment of our day is true prayer, at whatever level, how can we enter truly into prayer at any stated time? Jesus is not now 'yes' and now 'no' but always the eternal 'yes'. To yearn to be with him, that constant 'yes', our being itself crying in the Spirit to the Father, is not that the summary of prayer? Each level must have its part in our day and in a very real sense each is of equal value in that God is the value of our prayer—his the initiative, his the prime responsibility. If he chooses to love us when our attention is indirect as in the prayer of activity, then, though we may find this unsatisfying, it is the most to be valued because it is what God has chosen. Surely most of Jesus' day was spent thus? Perhaps it is only after long hours of practice in the selfless submission to what kind of prayer God chooses that we can give ourself wholly in pure prayer. This is the only prayer which by definition demands our undivided attention but the depth of that attention will be conditional on the fidelity with which we have let God possess us in indirect forms of prayer. Their value is not so much for what they are in themselves as what they effect in us, and from this angle they matter as much as the pure prayer from which alone they draw their generosity and to which they give value.

But perhaps we can add a fourth level of prayer which is really only a more intense form of pure prayer; the prayer of ecstasy. Petra claims a sort of absorption in pure prayer that never deprives her of consciousness. For ecstasy itself I rely on Claire. She describes it as 'light on' in its most intense form. To 'see' God means to be unable to see anything else, to think or move or do anything except receive what he is giving. The whole capacity of the person is filled to overflowing. But this has nothing to do with progress. The whole thing is God's, not the result of the soul having now come so close to him that this effect follows. God 'reveals' himself whenever he chooses and this tells us nothing about the individual's holiness. As we said earlier, ecstasy can happen at any stage and as it entails the whole being as seized by God, the effect on us will always be experienced as being the same; a full saucer must feel like a full bathtub.

Again it must be emphasised that what is experienced is not God, for God cannot be held within the limits of humanity. All the feelings and effects are on our side — the debris of the encounter — what is found left there when the visitor has gone. Thus they count for little except to hearten us.

Nowadays we know, as Teresa and John could not know, that similar psychic effects, which is all we can know intellectually of ecstasies, are produced equally and quite indistinguishably by purely natural means. How the person interprets these effects will depend upon her normal frame of reference: a religious person will see it as God and an atheist as some sort of nebulous insight into the nature of what-is. It could well be that many ecstasies are in fact natural phenomena, but the religious person thinking them of God receives them with reverence and humble joy and they become a genuine source of grace — God has used the mysterious workings of the unconscious to urge us on to greater generosity. So, though pride, obstinacy and the like are signs that God has not intervened, we cannot say the reverse, namely that good effects are signs that he has intervened in a supernatural or mystical way. It could well be grace coming in natural ways, as it usually does.

The distinguishing difference is interior change at depth, which is very hard to assess because the psychic effects can be so intense as to persuade us that we are changed in depth, and there may well be a true increase of generosity resulting from the shock of what was but a natural encounter. Only one who can discern the Spirit and who can observe over a long term can decide whether God has himself directly touched this person. He never does so without, spontaneously, his wisdom and essential love imprinting themselves. The whole thing is in a different dimension but only eyes at ease in that dimension can see it.

Why he should do this for someone is his secret. Perhaps to

accomplish what they could never do without this grace; perhaps just to enlighten others; perhaps just to be God to one who will let him be. Perhaps the role of the prophets in the old testament is the sign of his purpose. All their prophetic insight came from this mysterious contact which they could not hold but which left them wounded with God's being, as Jacob was.

Many words and sacred concepts have become debased: 'mystical' for instance. How far its truth lies from the romantic usage of the last century! 'Vision' is another such reality. I use the word 'reality' advisedly. A true vision does not belong to the peripheral area of the life of the spirit, such as the 'favours' which, throughout this book, we hold of small account. It belongs to the same category as ecstasy and, as Claire testifies, is a lesser form of it when God directs the dazzled gaze to one particular aspect of himself. But to repeat once again, in a true vision nothing is seen or can be seen; no eyes can enclose that essential and only true Vision. It will be recalled that St Teresa speaks of intellectual visions where nothing is seen either with the exterior or interior senses, nor in a conceptual way with the mind (VI mansion, 10). A true vision is an encounter in the depths of being. However, and this is where misunderstanding arises, a certain impress of this visitation has been left in a person and now they have to express this to themself. Yes, have to, for a vision is for use and has to have a comprehensible form. This is not the same for ecstasy, where a 'form' is not necessary; it is itself, its own value, its own point, so to speak. Thus someone has to search around their storehouse of images and symbols for something with which to fashion a substance and form for what has been seen in a totally non-conceptual way. This search and this fashioning will probably be done unconsciously, and this could account for the apparitions and imaginative visions Teresa gives us, or perhaps Bernadette of Lourdes. This task of giving comprehensible form to what is in itself formless is fraught with dangers, but less so of course when it is done consciously, with the realisation that the image presented is only a working model. Here is another place where historicity and environment will play a crucial role. Claire frequently has visions; she sees both people and general truths that God illuminates with himself, but to find words is almost impossible. Usually she feels the need to give an outline to what cannot even be glanced at but she is always conscious that this is tentative. She will carefully preface what she understands with 'I see this in him' to distinguish it from the products of her own natural insight and wisdom.

'Light off' has her own deep wisdom communicated direct from divine wisdom but, as Thérèse says, she finds it within her without knowing where it has come from. It seems like her own wisdom, flowing as it does through natural aqueducts. It is as truly God's wisdom as is that of visions, but in the latter case the subject of them is aware that God is here and now drawing her attention to what he would reveal to her. 'Light off' carries its own deep certainty, and yet perhaps in God's loving care for his children he knows that in our darkness and obscurity we need from time to time a flash of lightning to show us the truth of our truth, the certainty of what we know as certain. Blessed God!

From my knowledge of Claire I feel there is another deep reason why God occasionally destines a person to this 'light on' state. As I understand it, a 'light off' soul, that is one in the ordinary mystic way, enters into the human experience of Jesus in her own way. He lives in her what it is to be human. But there is another aspect of Jesus' human experience which she simply cannot share directly, that from God's point of view, so to speak. Not only did Jesus taste the bitterness of our human lot but he drank the chalice of his Father's grief, the awesome mystery of God's suffering love, love rejected. To share Jesus' cup one must 'see'. But one called to 'see' in this way can hardly live a normal life; it will inevitably be a rare vocation. Maybe we could sum up the two vocations in saying 'light on' shares Jesus' agony in the garden when he saw the reality of sin, seeing the Father's heart; 'light off' shares his utterly human experience when he hung in darkness on the cross, when he could not see his Father — the only time perhaps in his life when the light was off. The two experiences seem to be incompatible with one another, one must cancel out the other. Both are Jesus.

The wisdom of the transformed being is welling up from within, not flowing from without, yet I am always impressed by the way both Claire and Petra use their minds. It seems to me they are always pondering and reading, finding new insights in scripture as well as in a wide range of books. This is especially true of Claire, highly cultured woman that she is. Her mind, without the least impairment of its feminine intuitiveness, richness and delicacy, is masculine in its power, energy, thrust and boldness. She considers reading a vital part of her eremitical vocation; not a diversion or recreation, but an entering more deeply into the revelation of God in man and the world, a communion with others, and the development of herself as a person. Both Claire and Petra grasp that God asks this continual cultivation of their human powers so that he may glorify himself the more in them.

I came across the following letter written several years ago to Petra. It throws light on the function of the mind at this stage:

I can remember trying to teach the redemption according to Anselm, and the deadness of it. As more and more dogmatic knowledge came within the circle of his presence, it became lit up from within, and I could see for myself what was true of him, and what inadequate. But anything not in this circle was futile to me. I held on to it because of the church's authority, and it seems to me now that everything is either a revelation of him or else so opaque that I can tell it is not his revealed word but one of the accretions we were taught, like limbo, or the angelic hierarchy of nine etc. I think you are trying to speak of the same experience — that in some way God had made himself so real to you that no words or dogmatic formulae seemed anything but absurd. Mine was the same except that he always told me his name, whereas you 'knew' him in deeper obscurity. We were both living by this hidden knowledge, a living experience of God, but you could not drag this up to the mind's surface. All else was dim and unattractive because of it, just as for me.

It is generally accepted that those in the state of transforming union are confirmed in grace, that they cannot sin. This is simply explained. Looked at from their angle: throughout the long arduous journey across the second island they were unremittingly choosing God, saying 'yes' to every demand. Their whole being has, so to speak, set in that direction and cannot change; theoretically they can change but in fact they cannot. We find analogies in ordinary life. A woman brought up in a home and environment upholding the sanctity of marriage, practised in fidelity and self-giving, simply could not decide to break up the home and get out. In theory she could, yet we can at the same time quite confidently affirm that she couldn't. The same could be said of sets in bad directions. But there is the other side, God's. It has been mutual giving; continually he has drawn a person into himself and this embrace has evoked greater surrender. The time comes when he can take her completely, hold her so deeply and constantly within himself that she can go out no more.

How could she sin? God cannot fail himself. If by an impossibility she could break out of this blessed prison, then of course she would sin, but she cannot; her own structure, built of endless surrenders, and in God's safe keeping makes this impossible. This is another blessedness of this state, the certainty that one can never go back, that one is safe for ever; in a very real sense the goal is reached.

This does not mean such a person cannot grow or enter more deeply into God. There is still work to be done, but it is not a question of striving, for struggle is over, but rather deeper and deeper surrender, letting God do everything, and totally sure that he will do so. Again there is the blessedness of certitude. She cannot displease God, she is always his delight but she can please him less, so to speak, and this she must watch. It is probable that she could court death and God would grant her desire, because he will do all she wills, and she cannot will contrary to his will. All the same it could mean more to him to have her stay on earth, grow still more and give him greater love. It would seem probable that he would want her to remain on earth some time, perhaps many years. Nor is she perfect. The roots of sin are cut, but maybe some droopy little bits of green are still there—feelings of jealousy, annoyance, contrariness, but they are absolutely harmless, mere feelings, rather like those that remain when a limb has been amputated. She does not ask for them to go, because she knows they do not matter. Yes, she is not afraid to compare them with the wounds of Jesus, which still remain, tokens of a bloody struggle but a struggle that is over. She does not have to struggle against these feelings, they are there to keep her holding out her hand to Jesus.

I think this lowly note is the right one on which to stop discussion of a transformed being, affirming a holiness that is pure gift flowing over from him who alone is holy. Jesus is her holiness, and her holiness is human and not faultless. It is a holiness that accepts what man really is and what he must suffer, a holiness which is of non-alluring arduousness; Jesus made it clear to us. But we want a 'splendid way', a 'quick way', a 'way to keep our dignity and enhance it' while Jesus lived out a life of fundamental 'ordinariness'. Thérèse of Lisieux distinguished between her 'little way' for 'little souls' and the 'great way' for 'great souls' but there is no such 'great way' as there are no such 'great souls'. Thérèse in God's providence showed us the bare bones of holiness, and if there is holiness it is not because of 'greatness', high spiritual gifts, utmost generosity, ecstasies, visions, severe penance and so on — we have rather to speak of holiness in spite of these things — but because there is total acceptance of human lowliness and total surrender of it to God in trust. Claire and Petra are profoundly aware of this. If you like, Claire is a 'great soul' whereas Petra is one of Thérèse's legions of 'little ones' but Claire and Petra go the same way, each refusing to shelter behind 'generosity', penance, anything in fact. Claire has known the strong temptation to severe penance and resisted it, preferring to live in total exposure. Both look to God and not to self, they keep their eyes on him and live absolutely secure that he will show at each moment what he wants done, all of course in an ascetic framework. They understand that 'it is love I want, not sacrifice'. This is perfect liberty which is pure gift from him, and yet it is total surrender of all choice. Only when it happens can the paradox be understood. Seen from afar, the surrender, the nothing-for-self frightens people, in reality it is Jesus and his joy.

Just as we can say that one who has surrendered not merely loves but is love, so we can say that she is humility. It is not a case of the exercise of the virtue of humility but humility is her essence. Most of us can be humble at times, but it does not last.

Here humility is the mode of being. The self has dissolved around its burning centre, Christ, whose centre is the Father. Only he remains and any awareness of self that there is is unsubstantial, shadowy.

You alone are the holy one.